W9-ARU-768

PERGAMON INSTITUTE OF ENGLISH (NEW YORK)

Materials for Language Practice

READING SKILLS
FOR
THE FUTURE

OTHER TITLES IN THIS SERIES INCLUDE:

BATTAGLIA, John and Marilyn Fisher
* *Yoshi Goes to New York*
   Authentic discourse for listening comprehension

MATREYEK, Walter
Communicating in English: Examples and Models
   1. Functions
   2. Notions
   3. Situations

PINT, John
* *Pint's Passages for Aural Comprehension I*
   Twentieth Century News

* *Pint's Passages for Aural Comprehension II*
   Telephone Talk

* Includes audio cassette(s)

READING SKILLS
FOR
THE FUTURE

An intermediate workbook for reading comprehension

R. SUSAN LEBAUER

University of California at Irvine

PERGAMON PRESS

OXFORD · NEW YORK · TORONTO · SYDNEY · PARIS · FRANKFURT

U.K.	Pergamon Press Ltd., Headington Hill Hall, Oxford OX3 0BW, England
U.S.A.	Pergamon Press Inc., Maxwell House, Fairview Park, Elmsford, New York 10523, U.S.A.
CANADA	Pergamon Press Canada Ltd., Suite 104, 150 Consumers Road, Willowdale, Ontario M2J 1P9, Canada
AUSTRALIA	Pergamon Press (Aust.) Pty. Ltd., P.O. Box 544, Potts Point, N.S.W. 2011, Australia
FRANCE	Pergamon Press SARL, 24 rue des Ecoles, 75240 Paris, Cedex 05, France
FEDERAL REPUBLIC OF GERMANY	Pergamon Press GmbH, Hammerweg 6, D-6242 Kronberg-Taunus, Federal Republic of Germany

Copyright © 1983 Pergamon Press Ltd.

All Rights Reserved. No part of this publication may be reproduced, stored in a retrieval system or transmitted in any form or by any means: electronic, electrostatic, magnetic tape, mechanical, photocopying, recording or otherwise, without permission in writing from the publishers.

First edition 1983
Reprinted 1985

British Library Cataloguing in Publication Data
Lebauer, R. Susan
Reading skills for the future.—(Materials for
language practice)
1. English language—Text-books for foreigners
2. Readers—Science
I. Title II. Series.
428.6′4   PE1127.S3

ISBN 0-08-028619-4

A Flamm/Northam Book

Printed in Great Britain by A. Wheaton & Co. Ltd., Exeter

PREFACE

Reading Skills For The Future is a workbook designed to aid students to become more independent readers. This book will be especially interesting to those intermediate-level students planning to study in scientific or technical fields although any student desiring practice in reading factual material would find it useful. The book is divided into fourteen interrelated chapters. The student should never skip chapters, since important vocabulary and grammar points, once introduced, are practiced again and again in subsequent chapters.

Goals
I The student will increase his/her reading comprehension ability:
  A By increasing knowledge of grammatical points that show sentence or clause relationships (connectors, *just as . . . so is . . . , neither . . . nor . . .* , etc.)
  B By increasing knowledge of grammatical points that put the basic sentence into unfamiliar forms for the foreign reader (passive voice, defining and non-defining relative clauses, reduced relative clauses, etc.)
  C By increasing vocabulary:
    1. By learning the skills involved in using context clues
    2. By learning affixes and their meanings in order to make educated guesses about meaning
    3. By learning the dictionary skill of choosing the appropriate meaning out of many in a dictionary
  D By constantly testing pronoun referral understanding
  E By understanding paragraph organization:
    1. By learning how to write outlines
    2. By learning how to separate and group general ideas and details of paragraphs

3. By organizing sentences into logical paragraphs (paragraphs of chronological order, spatial order, comparison and justification) and learning the vocabulary that accentuates the paragraph organization

F By practicing direction-following and diagram-reading skills

II The student will be more confident in his/her ability to read material on his/her own.

ACKNOWLEDGEMENTS

This book is a revised and expanded version of materials that were first developed and implemented by a group made up of the author, Michael Giotis, Michael Grossman, and Pamela Pearson. The author would like to acknowledge the contributions of the three other members at that beginning stage.

The Publisher gratefully acknowledges the following sources of the visual materials in this book:

Chapter
1. National Coal Board (*Lea Hall Colliery, Rugeley, Staffs.*)
2. British Petroleum Co. Ltd. (*Production platform FA (Graythorpe)*)
3. Keystone Press Agency (*Desert*)
4. Central Electricity Generating Board (*Wylfa Nuclear Power Station*)
5. North of Scotland Hydro-Electric Board (*Cruachan Power Station, Argyll*)
6. Forestry Commission (*Thetford Forest*)
7. I.C.I. Plastics Division (*Solar Panels*)
8, 10, 11. Intermediate Technology Development Group (*Solar Water Heater, Methane Digester*)
9. British Gas Corporation (*Apollo II drilling rig*)
12. Nic Merrow-Smith (*Windmill*)
13. Central Electricity Generating Board (*Camarthen Bay Windmill*)
14. Central Electricity Generating Board (*Boeing MOD 2 wind turbine*)

Acknowledgement is also made to the following sources of the reading passages and cartoon:

Readings 9, 10, 11: Adapted by permission of Arusha Appropriate

Technology Project, Arusha, Tanzania.
Readings 12, 13, 14: Adapted from *Energy Book 1: National Sources and Backyard Applications*, edited by John Previs. Copyright © 1975 Running Press. Reprinted courtesy of Running Press, 38 South 19th Street, Philadelphia, PA, 19103.
Cartoon "Now?" by Bill Mauldin, by courtesy of Chicago Sun-Times.

CONTENTS

TO THE STUDENT

This book is called *Reading Skills For The Future* for two reasons:

1. **Your future:** This book is designed to give you the skills to become a more independent reader. It will help you eventually to read texts, technical manuals and general articles of your own choosing in your field.

2. **The world's future:** How much coal, oil, and gas remain? What will we do if we use up the earth's resources? Should we continue using energy as before or change our ways? These questions are of immediate concern to the world. This book contains thirteen readings pertaining to these questions. It includes readings about possible alternative energy systems, their good and bad points, and possible designs to use them.

THE TEACHER'S ROLE

Passage and worksheet

Each chapter contains a reading passage and a worksheet. (Chapter 1 is an exception and should be done with the students as a review.) The teacher should refrain from preparing the students for a reading. *There should be no advance work in vocabulary or subject-matter.* The goal is to have the student tackle the reading on his/her own.

All the information the student needs in order to analyze the passage is on the worksheet (i.e. vocabulary definitions, explanation of difficult sentences, and/or guides towards understanding difficult sentences). On the worksheet, the student will see and be asked to put into words all the ideas that readers normally process when reading. This includes paraphrasing sentences, breaking sentences down into simpler parts, making educated guesses about meanings from context, pinpointing important ideas and words in a passage, relating new ideas to ideas previously mentioned, and relating pronouns to the words they refer to.

Time-limits should not be placed on the worksheet. The teacher should get an idea of the range of his/her class. If one or two students are much slower than all of the others, mark the parts they finish and allow them to finish the rest at home. In general, though, this idea should be discouraged because the teacher can't be sure a student is working individually. For those students who finish before the rest, there are often additional assignments at the end of the worksheets. These are writing exercises and usually relate the student's background and experience to the passage just finished.

It would be a good idea for the teacher to correct the worksheet; however, he/she should not grade it. Simply identifying wrong answers would help both the student and teacher note areas of difficulty. During the next class, the teacher can go over the reading, the reading vocabulary and the worksheet, and give extra practice in words or areas of difficulty. At this point, the teacher can discuss the ideas in the reading to give oral practice in the vocabulary and to relate the reading to students' own ideas and so make the passage more 'alive' to them.

Vocabulary exercises

Most chapters contain a vocabulary exercise. The students are asked either to fill in a blank or replace an italicized word with a synonym using a new vocabulary word. Of the two exercise types, the former is more difficult but gives the student the opportunity to practice more language skills. The teacher should direct the students in the steps involved in filling in the blanks by asking:

'What kind of word belongs here?' (adjective, noun, etc.)
'What idea belongs here?'
'What word in the vocabulary list matches that idea? Is it in the correct form?'

In this way, the student is given practice in using context clues and root derivations as well as simple new vocabulary practice.

Affix exercises

Students are given lists of affixes, examples of their use, and their meanings. The students can fill in the blanks on the affix charts using simple logic. Exercises follow the chart. The teacher should give additional practice in sentence formation with words and their derivations, and additional examples as needed. Whenever an affix comes up in class, the teacher should point it out and allow students to guess at the possible definition.

Outlines

The outlines expected from the students get progressively more difficult. At the beginning, the blanks left in the outline can be deduced easily using the information already given in the outline. This shows the students the logic inherent in an outline because they are relating the parts they must supply to those already given. Later on, the students must use the passage and their own sense of logic, as less information will be given by the author.

The teacher can demonstrate the usefulness of outlines by asking the students to (1) tell the class, in one sentence, what the passage is about (they will have to look at the roman numerals on their outlines), (2) tell the class the main ideas in the story (they will probably look at the roman numerals and capital letters), and (3) describe the passage in detail (they will use the whole outline).

The teacher should encourage different outlines and stress that each student *interprets* readings as an individual. The teacher must make sure that the sequence of the outline is logical and that ideas of the same degree of generality are grouped together.

Paragraph organization exercises

The student is asked to order a group of sentences into a logical paragraph. Most important, the student must choose the topic sentence, or most general sentence, out of the group. The student should then decide how the remaining sentences relate to the topic sentence. Allow students to discuss differing viewpoints. Again, different answers may be acceptable as long as they are logical in the teacher's eyes.

These exercises also include words and phrases that serve to accentuate the relations between sentences, e.g. *subsequently, prior to* and *in contrast*. These words should be pointed out as key words. As the students' speed increases, they will need to be able to discriminate between the words which give a lot of information and those that can be skimmed. A good exercise is to have the students underline the vocabulary that helped them to order the sentences.

Grammar exercises

This book is by no means a grammar book. The grammar points focused on are chosen because they seem to be essential to reading comprehension. The passive voice and relative clauses receive attention because they change the familiar basic sentence into an unfamiliar form for the foreign reader. In addition, the passive voice and relative clauses especially abound in technical literature.

The grammar in this book is in condensed form. The exercises are designed to find particular problems. This book should not introduce the grammar. The teacher should introduce the grammar point and practice it with the class. Then the students can read the explanation and do the exercises as a review and confirmation of their understanding. By looking at the students' mistakes, the teacher should be able to judge their areas of difficulty. Grammar is taught in this book as an aid to reading comprehension. It is not taught for production purposes. The teacher may supplement this material with production practice, if desired.

Certain exercises in judging defining and non-defining relative clauses may have two answers. Allow the students to argue their viewpoint. By defending their views, the students will see that much of reading depends on interpretation. They will also see that small differences in punctuation and word order can change meaning drastically.

Additional activities
Encourage involvement in the reading material. Students should be actively participating in reading and discussing the reading. Encourage students to go beyond the simple examples of appropriate technology in this book. Activities can include going to the library and looking up books and other material on appropriate technology projects. In addition, trips to working projects may be planned. Allow students to research the pros and cons of different forms of energy. Organize debates in class. Hopefully, the students will finish this book with a feeling of having acquired useful, relevant information about the world around them as well as a better command of the English language.

CHAPTER 1

Grammar Review

I Sentence parts

   A Verbs

   B Subjects

   C Objects

   D Complements

   E Predicates

   F Auxiliaries

II Sentence types

   A Basic sentences

     1. Subject, verb, object, complement

     2. More than one subject, object, or complement (using *and* or *or*)

     3. Negative sentences

   B Compound predicate sentences (joined by *and* or *or*)

Reading 1: About this book

(1) This book contains readings about energy. (2) Through these readings, you will practice finding general ideas and details in paragraphs. (3) You will increase your reading comprehension, your grammar, and your vocabulary. (4) Your teacher will help you individually. (5) You will do most of the work by yourself.

(6) This reading is very easy. (7) The rest of the book is not like this. (8) It will become much more difficult.

Look at the kinds of sentence in this reading. What do they have in common? They are all *basic sentences*.

A basic sentence may be a statement (.), a question (?), or an exclamation (!). It always begins with a capital letter and ends with some sort of punctuation. Each sentence contains a subject, a verb and an optional object and/or complement.

A *verb* is a word or words which express an action or state of being.

Exercise 1 *Underline each verb in the reading.*
How many verbs does a basic sentence have? ....

A *subject* is the thing or person that is doing the action (the actor).

Exercise 2 *Put two lines under the subject in each sentence.*

An *object* is the thing or person that is receiving the action. A *complement* may be an adjective or an adjectival clause (a word or group of words describing the subject or object) or an adverb or adverbial clause (a word or group of words describing the verb).

Exercise 3 *Circle the object or complement in each sentence.*

Example (1) This book contains (readings) about energy.

Look at sentence (5). There is an object and a complement. What is the order?

subject	verb	object	complement
	predicate		

3

The *predicate* includes everything except the subject.

Exercise 4 *Rearrange these three groups of words into sentences. Underline the predicate in each group.*

1. will see	after class	the teacher	us
2. reads	books	by himself	he
3. are taking	the students	notes	from the readings

....

....

....

....

....

....

....

Look at sentence (2) in the reading. How many direct objects are there? .... What about sentence (3)? .... We can also write basic sentences in these forms. Notice that there is still only one verb.

subject   verb $\left\{\begin{array}{l}\text{object}\\\text{object and/or object}\\\text{object, object and/or object}\end{array}\right\}$ complement

'You will do most of the work by yourself, with a partner, or in a group.' In this sentence, we have more than one complement. It has the same form as the multiple object.

$\left\{\begin{array}{l}\text{complement}\\\text{complement and/or complement}\\\text{complement, complement and/or complement}\end{array}\right\}$

Do you think that we can have more than one subject? 'You and your class-mates will practice finding general ideas and details in paragraphs.' Again, this has the same form as the multiple object and complement.

Exercise 5 *Write a complete chart (combining the ones above) to show basic sentence structure and word order. (Show possible multiple subjects, objects, and complements.)*

Exercise 6 *Change the sentences in the story to their negative form.* Remember that every negative question or statement must have an auxiliary. If there is no auxiliary, you must supply one. The negative always follows the auxiliary. Here is a list of auxiliaries:

am, is, are, were, was, did, do, does, has, have, had, can, could should, will, would, shall, might, may, must, ought

....

....

....

....

....

Exercise 7 *Combine sentences (2) and (3) with* and. *Do not repeat words that are not necessary.*

....

....

....

You have now formed a sentence with two predicates (a *compound predicate sentence*), but still only one subject. The subject is the same in both clauses but the verbs are different. This is a good way to join sentences having the same subject. The two predicates can be joined by *and* or *or. Combine sentences (2) and (5) with* and.

....

....

....

....

Exercise 8 *From this list of words, form as many sentences as you can in five minutes.*

they	their	its	are	our	students
use	scientists	coal	study	uses	properties
gas	and	of	farmers		

Score yourself as follows:

1 subject, 1 verb, 1 object or complement	→ 1 point
1 subject, 1 verb, 2 objects or complements	→ 2 points
2 subjects, 1 verb, 1 object or complement	→ 2 points
3 subjects, 1 verb, 2 objects or complements	→ 3 points
1 subject, 2 predicates	→ 4 points

CHAPTER 2

Vocabulary

present	to exhaust
to paraphrase	decade
composition/decomposition	to decide
organic	to make a decision
to predict	to affect
to make a prediction	within (*time period*)

Affixes

Prefix *de-* (opposite process)

Grammar

I Sentence types

  A Compound sentences

    1. With co-ordinate conjunctions
      (a) *and*
      (b) *but*
      (c) *so*

    2. With replacements for coordinate conjunctions

Reading 2: Our energy resources

(1) Our present-day energy supply consists largely of fossil fuels. (2) Fossil fuels are fuels that are formed by the decomposition of organic materials. (3) They include coal, oil, and gas.

(4) We started using these fossil fuels in large quantities less than 200 years ago and we haven't stopped since. (5) Some scientists are now predicting that we will exhaust our supplies of fossil fuels within five decades. (6) We didn't have a problem 200 years ago, but we do now.

(7) Some people say, 'Live for today,' but others think that we should look ahead to the future. (8) The decision we make about energy today will affect the world's future, so we should decide carefully. (9) Should we look for new energy supplies (such as the sun, wind, water, and atomic energy) or should we 'live for today' and 'forget about tomorrow'?

Worksheet

Do the following worksheet after reading the passage to yourself.

Check the right answers.

Sentence 1

1. 'Our present-day energy supply' means:
   (a) The energy supply which we use presently (nowadays) ☐
   (b) The energy supply that is available during the day ☐
   (c) The energy supply which we are given as presents ☐

To paraphrase is to say a sentence in a different way. Sometimes we break the sentence down into smaller sentences. Sometimes we change the vocabulary. It is a good way to make a sentence clearer and also to make sure that you understand the meaning.

2. A paraphrase of sentence (1) is:
   (a) Our present energy supply is made up of fossil fuels that are bigger than usual. ☐
   (b) Our present energy supply is mostly made up of fossil fuels. ☐
   (c) Our energy supply during the day is mostly made up of fossil fuels. ☐

Sentence 2

Organic materials are materials that contain the element carbon (C). *Composition* is the act of putting together the parts of a whole.

1. *De-* is a prefix which means to do the opposite process. What does *decomposition* mean? ....

   ....

   ....

   ....

2. Organic materials include:
   (a) A light bulb ☐
   (b) A teapot ☐
   (c) Plants and animals ☐

11

Sentence 4

1. Here is a time chart. Color in the period of use of fossil fuels in large quantities.

400 years ago   200 years ago   present   future

2. We started using these fossil fuels in large quantities 200 years ago, and we haven't stopped .... since.
   What words were omitted to make the sentence shorter?

Sentence 5

To *predict* is to tell something about the future; to make a prediction.
To *exhaust* means to finish; to use up.
A *decade* is 10 years.

1. 'Within five decades' means:
   (a) Five decades exactly (50 years)
   (b) More than five decades
   (c) Five decades or less

2. A paraphrase of sentence (5) is:
   (a) Fossil fuels will make scientists tired within 50 years.
   (b) Scientists will use up all of our fossil fuels within 50 years.
   (c) Within 50 years, scientists say that our fossil fuel supply might be finished.

Sentence 6

1. We didn't have a problem 200 years ago, but we do

   .... now.
   What words were omitted to shorten the sentence?

Sentence 7

1. Another way to say 'live for the present' is

   ....
2. Which sentence is true?
   (a) A person who 'lives for today' will reduce his use of fossil fuels because we may soon exhaust our supply.

(b) A person who looks ahead to the future will use the same amount of fossil fuels because we may soon exhaust our supply. ☐

(c) A person who 'lives for today' will use the same amount of fossil fuels because he does not care that we may soon exhaust our supply. ☐

Sentence 8

1. The noun form of *decide* is *decision*. We say 'make a prediction'.

   We also say '............................. decision'.

To *affect* means to have an influence on.

Sentence 9

1. Answer the question in sentence (9) beginning with 'We should look for new energy supplies because . . .' or 'We should live for today and forget about tomorrow because . . .'.

   ....

   ....

APPLY YOUR KNOWLEDGE *This question is for those students who have finished the worksheet before the others in the class.*

Are you a person who 'lives for today' or are you a person who 'lives for tomorrow'? Give examples of how you are one or the other from events in your life.

....

....

....

....

....

....

....

Grammar

Look at sentences (4), (6), (7) and (8). How many basic sentences are in each sentence? .... These sentences which are made up of more than one basic sentence are called *compound sentences*. A compound sentence contains two *clauses*. A clause contains a subject and a verb but it doesn't stand alone; it is part of a longer sentence.

In sentences (4), (6), (7) and (8), which words join the two clauses? .... These words are called *coordinate conjunctions*. They join two related sentences. Do not join sentences that have no relationship.

Exercise 1 What is the relationship of sentences joined by *but*? *But* connects two sentences with contrasting ideas. *Finish the following sentences with logical second clauses*:

1. I failed the last test but ....

2. I didn't come to class yesterday but ....

3. We didn't have an energy crisis 200 years ago but

....

What is the relationship of sentences joined by *so*? *So* connects a sentence which states a reason to a sentence which states a result. In sentence (8), where is the reason clause?

....;

the result clause? ....

Why should we decide carefully about energy? (Look for the answer in the reason clause.)

....

Finish the following sentences with a logical second clause:

4. I failed the first test so ....

14

5. I didn't come to school yesterday so ....

....

6. We didn't have an energy crisis 200 years ago so ....

....

When we connect two sentences with *and*, we add more information about something in the first clause. *Finish the following sentences with logical second clauses:*

7. I failed the first test and ....

8. I didn't come to school yesterday and ....

....

9. We didn't have an energy crisis 200 years ago and

....

Many words are used which have the same meaning as the coordinate conjunctions. Some possible substitutions are:

and (clause 1 *and* clause 2 which adds extra information)
  Fossil fuels are becoming expensive, *and* we are exhausting our supplies of them.
  Fossil fuels are becoming expensive; { furthermore, } we are { in addition, }
exhausting our supplies of them.

so (reason clause *so* result clause)
  Fossil fuels may soon be exhausted, *so* we should look for new supplies of energy.
  Fossil fuels may soon be exhausted; { therefore, / thus, / for this reason, / consequently, / as a result, } we

should look for new sources of energy.

but (clause 1 *but* clause 2 which qualifies or limits the first clause)
  Fossil fuels may soon be exhausted *but* some people continue to use large amounts of them carelessly.

15

Fossil fuels may soon be exhausted; { however, nevertheless, } some people continue to use large amounts carelessly.

but (clause 1 *but* clause 2 which contrasts with the first clause)
As industry develops, our world needs more and more energy, *but* as time passes, our supplies of energy get smaller and smaller.
As industry develops, our world needs more and more energy;
{ on the other hand, in contrast, on the contrary, whereas,* } as time passes, our supplies of energy get smaller and smaller.

*   *preceded by a comma*

Exercise 2 *Look back to sentences (4), (6), (7) and (8). Replace the coordinate conjunctions with these new words orally in class.*
    Example (Sentence (4)) We started using these fossil fuels in large quantities less than 200 years ago; furthermore, we haven't stopped since then.

Exercise 3 *Look at the following pairs of sentences. Decide which coordinate conjunction could best join them. Then choose another possible word from the words on the preceding pages.*
    Example Oil is going to be more and more expensive.
                Heating with oil is going to cost more.
    Answer Oil is going to be more and more expensive, so heating with oil is going to cost more.
             Oil is going to be more and more expensive; for this reason, heating with oil is going to cost more.

1. Exhausting our fuel supply will stop industry all over the world. We should try to find new supplies of energy now before it is too late.

    ....

    ....

2. We should reduce our use of fossil fuels. Many people are increasing their use every day.

    ....

    ....

3. Fossil fuels were found in large quantities 200 years ago.
   Our present supply is found in smaller quantities.

   ....

   ....

4. Oil is found in the Middle East.
   Oil is found in South America.

   ....

   ....

5. As the supply of oil gets smaller, oil gets more expensive.
   We should find new energy supplies that are cheaper and in large
   supply.

   ....

   ....

6. Engineers build constructions to produce energy.
   Engineers should be interested in the growing problems of energy
   supplies.

   ....

   ....

7. People know that our supplies of fossil fuels may soon be exhausted.
   They continue to build constructions which use them.

   ....

   ....

8. Fossil fuels are used by individuals to cook with and to heat houses
   and water.
   They are used by industries to provide power to run machinery.

   ....

   ....

KSFTF–B

CHAPTER 3

Vocabulary

crisis	bound	to alternate
to hit hard	poverty	alternative
rural	to meet basic needs	source
urban	majority	potential
developing countries	to get attention	resources
available	to pay attention	concentration
to search	to satisfy needs	to concentrate
crops	reasonable	generally
income	to conserve	to extract
fertilizers	conservation	effort
scarce	to benefit	

Affixes

Suffixes that change adjectives or verbs to nouns (*-or, -ness, -ment, -ity, -ation, -ion, -tion, -sion, -ce, -ence*)

Grammar

I Sentence types
  A Sentences with *because* (result clause *because* reason clause)
  B Passive voice

Reading 3: The energy crisis

(1) The energy crisis hits hardest at rural families in developing countries because they have the least energy available to them. (2) It means that they have to walk further and search harder for firewood and water. (3) It means poorer crops and lower incomes because fertilizers have become scarce and expensive. (4) It means that, more than ever, they are bound to poverty, and that their basic needs are not met.

(5) Rural people in developing countries make up the majority of the world's population; however, their energy needs get little attention. (6) Engineers should try to satisfy these needs at a reasonable cost. (7) To help meet rural agricultural energy needs, they should practice conservation and search for alternative sources of energy supplies.

(8) Sunlight, wind, and water have the potential to provide thousands of times more energy than the world presently uses. (9) Furthermore, it is the rural areas of developing countries that generally have the largest concentrations of these resources. (10) We must extract that energy and provide it in useful forms when and where it is needed. (11) This is necessary in any future development efforts to benefit rural families.

Worksheet

Sentence 1

A *crisis* is a major problem.

1. If someone hits your arm hard, how will it feel?
   (a) It will feel good. ☐
   (b) It will hurt. ☐
   Therefore, *to hit hard* is a *synonym* (a word which means the same

   as another word) of .... or *to affect*.

2. Paris, New York, and Tokyo are not rural areas. They are *urban* areas. What are some characteristics of these places?

   ....
   A *rural* area is the opposite. What are some rural areas in your country? What are some characteristics of these rural areas?

   ....

Developing countries are countries that are just beginning to use and develop modern technologies.

3. Which of the following are developing countries?
   (a) Afghanistan ☐
   (b) USA ☐
   (c) USSR ☐
   (d) Bangladesh ☐

4. 'They' refers to:
   (a) The energy crisis ☐
   (b) Rural families in developing countries ☐
   (c) Developing countries ☐

Available means capable of being used; usable.

5. In compound sentences with *because*, does the reason clause or

   the result clause follow *because*? .... Why does the energy crisis hit hardest at rural families in developing countries?

   ....

Which is the reason clause in sentence (1)?

....

6. In the last lesson we learned that sentences with *so* had the follow-
    ing order: reason clause *so* result clause. Which of the following is
    a paraphrase of sentence (1)?
    (a) The energy crisis hits hardest at rural families in de-
         veloping countries so they have the least energy avail-
         able to them.   ☐
    (b) So they have the least energy available to them, the
         energy crisis hits hardest at rural families in developing
         countries.   ☐
    (c) Rural families in developing countries have the least
         energy available to them so the energy crisis hits them
         hardest.   ☐

Sentence 2

1. 'It' refers to:
    (a) The energy crisis   ☐
    (b) Rural families   ☐
    (c) Developing countries   ☐

2. 'They' refers to:
    (a) The energy crisis   ☐
    (b) Rural families in developing countries   ☐
    (c) Developing countries   ☐

To *search* means to look for.

Sentence 3

Crops are plants grown on a farm.
Income is money coming in (or salary).
Fertilizers are substances used to make soil more productive.
Scarce means rare.

1. What is the result of fertilizers becoming scarce and more expensive?

....

Sentence 4

Bound means tied; held tightly.
Poverty is the noun form of *poor*. It is the state of being poor.

To meet basic needs means to provide basic needs; to satisfy basic needs.

1. A paraphrase of sentence (4) is:
   (a) The energy crisis means that rural families are tied to their farms. Because they are tied, these families cannot go to the store to get what they need. ☐
   (b) Developing countries mean that rural families will always be poor and that they will never be provided with their basic needs. ☐
   (c) It will be hard for rural families to be free from poverty. It also means that they will not receive enough things like food, clothes and a house. ☐

Sentence 5

Majority means large percentage.
To get attention means to receive notice; to be noticed.
To pay attention means to notice.

1. Which of the following sentences is true?
   (a) Rural families pay little attention to their energy needs. ☐
   (b) Energy needs get little attention from rural people. ☐
   (c) People do not pay attention to the energy needs of rural people. ☐

2. What word or words could replace 'however'? ....

Sentence 6

To satisfy needs means to give people enough of what they need.
Reasonable means with reason or logical.

1. A 'reasonable cost' would be:
   (a) A higher cost than necessary ☐
   (b) A lower cost than necessary ☐
   (c) A cost that is neither higher nor lower than necessary ☐

Sentence 7

1. If 'meeting basic needs' means to satisfy the demand for the basic things in life (food, home, etc.), what does 'meeting rural agricultural energy needs' mean?

   ....

Conserve means to save. *Conservation* means the act of saving. When we talk about energy conservation, it means saving energy and not wasting it.

The verb *to alternate* means to change. An *alternative* is a change or another possibility. It can be an adjective or a noun.

2. In the reading, we speak of 'alternative supplies'. Here, is 'alternative' an adjective or a noun? .... What does 'alternative

   supplies' mean? ....

A *source* is a beginning or a place where something comes from.

Sentence 8

Potential means capability.

Sentence 9

1. A synonym for 'furthermore' is ....
2. What is the relationship between sentences (8) and (9)?
   (a) Sentence (9) adds extra information concerning sentence (8). ☐
   (b) Sentence (9) contrasts with sentence (8). ☐
   (c) Sentence (9) is the result; sentence (8) is the reason. ☐

Resources are available supplies.

3. What does 'these resources' refer to?

   ....

To concentrate means to place or find in large amounts. A *concentration* is a point where something is found in large amounts.
Generally means usually.

Sentence 10

To extract means to remove; to take out.

1. What does 'it' refer to? ....
2. A paraphrase of sentence (10) is:
   (a) If we want to help rural families, we should find ways to make energy from the sun, wind, and water usable. We

should find ways to make it available at the times and places it is needed most. ☐

(b) We should find ways to remove sun, wind, and water from rural areas. We should then bring it to different places where it is needed ☐

(c) If we want to help rural families, we should provide them with more sunlight, wind, and water. ☐

Sentence 11

An *effort* is a try, an attempt.
To benefit someone is to do good for someone.

APPLY YOUR KNOWLEDGE *These questions are for those students who have finished the worksheet before the others in the class.*

1. What do you think basic needs are? What can you (in your profession) do to provide them to others?

   ....

   ....

2. Do you think rural people get less attention than urban people? Give your reasons.

   ....

   ....

Review questions for discussion

1. Who does the energy crisis affect the most? How does it affect them?
2. What are some possible ways to meet rural agricultural energy needs?
3. What are some alternative sources of energy?
4. Why would these alternative sources especially benefit rural people?
5. What must we learn to do before we can use these alternative sources?

Vocabulary

Fill in the blanks with words from the vocabulary list at the beginning of this chapter. First think about what idea would be logical in the blank left in the sentence. Think about what part of speech the missing word must be (verb, noun, etc.). Then look for a vocabulary word that matches the idea.

1. If there is a .... in your family, you must hurry home and help.

2. Gold is ....; therefore, it is expensive.

3. If you spend more money than your ...., you will have to borrow money.

4. The .... of people in Saudi Arabia are Moslems.

5. If we don't like the possibilities, we should look for ....

Rewrite the following sentences replacing the words in italics with words(s) from the reading which mean the same thing.

6. A shortage (a small supply) of teachers and materials *affects* students *the most*.

   A shortage of teachers and materials .... at students.

7. It is getting harder and harder to find new sources of energy but we have to continue to *look* for them.

   ....

8. Most children have the *capability* to learn to read.

   ....

9. Most people do not *notice* the rural areas because they are poor and don't have a large concentration of people.

   ....

10. Good doctors and medicine *do good for* old and sick people.

   ....

Grammar—passive voice

Two different types of sentence are *passive sentences* and *active sentences*.

Active sentences

| I | see | the | man. | | We | should | practice | conservation. |

| subject (actor) | verb | object (receiver of action) | | subject (actor) | verb | object (receiver of action) |

These sentences can be paraphrased in the passive voice:

Passive Voice sentences

The man was seen by me.   Conservation should be practiced by us.

| (receiver of action) | verb | (actor) | | (receiver of action) | verb | (actor) |

In a passive sentence, the receiver of the action (the object of the active sentence) is most important and the actor (the subject of the active sentence) is less important and sometimes unknown. Therefore, the receiver of the action comes first and the actor comes last in a passive sentence.

The actor in a passive sentence, if there is one, is always preceded by *by*.

The verb also changes in a passive sentence. In a passive sentence, the verb always has a form of *to be* and the past participle of the main verb. By looking at the verb, we can tell if a sentence is passive or active.

Here is a chart of the transformation from active to passive:

Active	actor (subject)	verb	receiver of action (object)
Passive	receiver of action	verb (*to be* + past participle)	by	actor

Look at this sentence: 'Rural families' basic needs are not met.' Is this a passive or an active sentence? .... Underline the receiver of the action. Is there an actor? .... This is an example where the actor is not known. To paraphrase this sentence in the active form, we must rearrange the actor and the receiver of the action and change the verb. We can add a general actor (*someone*) because there is none in this sentence. We put the actor first, then the verb, and then the receiver of the action to form an active sentence. 'Someone does not meet rural families' basic needs.' You can see that this sentence is more logical in the passive voice.

Look at sentence (10): 'We must extract that energy and provide it in useful forms when and where it is needed.' Underline the passive verb in this sentence. (Remember that in a passive construction the verb must have a form of *to be* + *past participle*). What is the receiver of the action of this verb? .... (Remember that in a passive voice construction the receiver of the action comes before the verb.) Is there an actor? .... Use *someone* and change this sentence to its active form.

....

Only the part of the sentence with the passive construction changes. The rest of the sentence remains the same. 'We must extract that energy and provide it in useful forms when and where *someone needs it.*' (The verb is in the present tense because we have 'is needed' in the passive construction: *is* is the present tense form of *to be*.)

Exercise

1. A paraphrase of sentence (6) ('Engineers should try to satisfy these needs at a reasonable cost') is:
   (a) These needs should be satisfied by engineers at a reasonable cost. ☐
   (b) These needs at a reasonable cost should satisfy engineers. ☐
   (c) These needs should be satisfy engineers at a reasonable cost. ☐
   (d) At a reasonable cost, should be satisfied by engineers these needs. ☐

2. A paraphrase of 'We should search for alternative sources of energy supplies' (sentence 7) is:
   (a) Alternative sources of energy supplies should be searched for by us. ☐
   (b) Alternative sources should be search by us of energy supplies. ☐
   (c) Energy supplies should be searches by us for alternative sources. ☐
   (d) Alternative sources of energy supplies should is searched for by us. ☐

3. A paraphrase of 'Fossil fuels may soon be exhausted' is:
   (a) Someone may soon exhausted fossil fuels. ☐
   (b) Someone may soon exhaust fossil fuels. ☐
   (c) Someone may soon be exhausted by fossil fuels. ☐
   (d) Fossil fuels may soon exhaust. ☐
Is the passive or active voice of this sentence more logical?

....

4. A paraphrase of 'Fossil fuels are formed by the decomposition of organic materials' is:
   (a) The decomposition formed fossil fuels of organic materials. ☐
   (b) Fossil fuels form the decomposition of organic materials. ☐
   (c) The decomposition of organic materials are formed fossil fuels. ☐
   (d) The decomposition of organic materials forms fossil fuels. ☐

5. A paraphrase of 'We used fossil fuels 200 years ago for the new developing industries' is:
   (a) Fossil fuels 200 years ago for the new developing industries were used by us. ☐
   (b) Fossil fuels were used by us 200 years ago for the new developing industries. ☐
   (c) Fossil fuels are used by us 200 years ago for the new developing industries. ☐
   (d) Fossil fuels were use by us 200 years ago for the new developing industries. ☐

6. A paraphrase of 'Fossil fuels are being used carelessly by individuals and industries' is:
   (a) Individuals and industries are using fossil fuels carelessly. ☐
   (b) Individuals are using fossil fuels and industries care-
       lessly. ☐
   (c) Carelessly are using fossil fuels by individuals and
       industries. ☐
   (d) Individuals and industries used fossil fuels carelessly. ☐

7. A paraphrase of 'A crisis will be caused by an energy shortage' is:
   (a) An energy shortage causes a crisis. ☐
   (b) A crisis will cause an energy shortage. ☐
   (c) A crisis causes an energy shortage. ☐
   (d) An energy shortage will cause a crisis. ☐

8. A paraphrase of 'Saudi Arabia produces a large percentage of our
   fossil fuel supply' is:
   (a) A large percentage of our fossil fuel supply produces
       Saudi Arabia. ☐
   (b) A large percentage of our fossil fuel supply produced by
       Saudi Arabia. ☐
   (c) A large percentage of our fossil fuel supply is produced
       by Saudi Arabia. ☐
   (d) Saudi Arabia is produced by a large percentage of our
       fossil fuel supply. ☐

Suffixes

Suffixes are letters which are added to the end of a word to change the meaning or part of speech of that word. In the reading, you saw words like 'conserve', 'conservation', 'concentrate', 'concentration', 'exhaust', 'exhaustion', 'decide', 'decision', 'predict' and 'prediction'. This is the suffix *-tion, -ation, -sion* and *-ion*. It changes verbs to nouns.

Here is a list of other suffixes which form nouns out of adjectives or verbs. *Complete the blanks in the chart.*

Root	*Suffix*	*Noun*
to work	-er	worker (one who works)
....	-er	teacher (.........................)
sad	-ness	sadness (the state of being sad; the quality of being sad)
soft	-ness	.... (..)
....	-ness	happiness (...)
to agree	-ment	agreement (concrete result of agreeing)
to achieve	-ment	.... (..)
to amaze	-ment	amazement (state of being amazed)
to enjoy	-ment	.... (state of enjoying)
creative	-ity	creativity (quality of being creative)
acidic, acid	-ity	acidity (quality of being like an acid)
to conserve	-ation	conservation (action or process of conserving)
to dehydrate	-ion	dehydration (action or process of dehydrating)
to calculate	-ion	.... (..)
to construct	-ion	construction (something constructed)
to relate	-ion	.... (..)
to attract	-ion	attraction (something that attracts)

to direct	-ion	direction (...)
to produce	-tion	production (something produced)
....	-tion	reduction (the process of reducing; the amount by which something is reduced)
to extend	-sion	extension (something that extends)
patient	-ce	patience (the state of being patient)
....	-ance	resistance (the state of resisting)

Note: -ation, -tion, -sion, and -ion are all the same suffix, which changes depending on the letters or syllables which precede it.

Exercise *Fill in the blanks using the correct form of the word given.*

1. (*exhaust*) The possible .... of fossil fuels affects us all.

2. (*conserve*) In order to .... energy, we can drive our cars less.

3. (*construct*) Engineers build .... that use fossil fuels.

4. (*reduce*) If we .... our use of fossil fuels, we may not have a problem in fifty years.

5. (*agree*) Scientists .... that fossil fuels will not last forever.

6. (*agree*) However, they are not in .... about when they will be exhausted.

7. (*creative*) Scientists will have to be .... in order to think up new ways to conserve energy.

8. (*concentrate*) Our present day fossil fuel supplies are

   .... in the Middle East.

9. (*patient*) We do not have the time to be .... with people who use fossil fuels carelessly.

10. (*reduce*) A small .... in gasoline usage might make a difference.

CHAPTER 4

Vocabulary

to civilize	to depend on something	dependence
civilization	complacent	to lead
to trace	renewable	situation
to domesticate	heed/heedless	to be beyond one's reach
milestone	to maintain/maintenance	to draw
domestication	world-wide	internal/external
dramatic	demands	interior/exterior
industrial	feasible/unfeasible	tides
fossil fuels	to be dependent on something	wisely
abundant		

Affixes

Suffixes that change roots to adjectives (-*al, -ive, -ous, -ful, -less, -able, -like*)

Grammar

 I Summarizing paragraphs in one sentence

II Outlines

Reading 4: Alternative energy

(1) The development of civilization can be traced through the story of man's discovery and use of new energy sources. (2) The discovery of fire, the domestication of animals, the development of agriculture, the invention of the steam engine, and the use of coal and oil are all important milestones. (3) Each milestone has brought about a dramatic change in man's way of life.

(4) We are now beginning to change from oil, coal, and gas to new sources of energy. (5) Our industrial civilization was built on abundant supplies of fossil fuels; for this reason, it now depends on them. (6) Still, we must not become complacent, because fossil fuels are not renewable. (7) Heedless use will soon exhaust our energy resources and leave us without the energy to maintain our civilization. (8) This problem is world-wide and affects all civilizations. (9) In both developed and developing countries, increasing costs of fossil fuels (because of limited supplies and high demands) often make projects which use them economically unfeasible. (10) Dependence on fossil fuels also leads to world-wide dependence on a limited number of countries. (11) This situation is a growing problem.

(12) Solutions to our energy problems are not beyond our reach. (13) We have the knowledge and the ability to draw energy from the sun, water, the wind, the tides, and the internal heat of the earth. (14) The use of atomic energy is also a possibility. (15) During the next few decades we will have to learn to use energy more wisely while at the same time new energy sources are developed.

Worksheet

Sentence 1

1. What are the two parts (a root, a suffix) in 'development'?

   .... What part of speech is 'development'?

   ....

2. What are the two parts in 'civilization'? (To *civilize* means to reach

   a higher state of culture and technology.) ....

   What part of speech is 'civilization'? ....

To trace means to follow; to follow a development.

3. Which is *not* a paraphrase of sentence (1)?
   (a) We can follow the development of civilization if we trace the story of man's discovery and use of new energy sources. ☐
   (b) We can be followed by the development of civilization if we trace the story of man's discovery and use of new energy sources. ☐
   (c) By following the story of man's discovery and use of new energy sources, we can see the development of civilization. ☐

Sentence 2

To domesticate means to make something usable by man; to tame.

1. 'Domestication' is:
   (a) One who domesticates ☐
   (b) The quality of being domesticated ☐
   (c) The action or process of domesticating ☐
2. 'Invention' is:
   (a) One who invents ☐
   (b) The quality of inventing ☐
   (c) Something that is invented ☐

To invent is to form something different or new.
A *milestone* is an important moment; an important event.

Sentence 3

Dramatic means noticeable; having a great effect.

PARAGRAPH 1
1. Which of the following *best* summarizes paragraph (1)?
    (a) Tracing the development of civilization through the discovery and use of new energy sources ☐
    (b) Dramatic changes in men's lives ☐
    (c) The discovery of fire ☐

Sentence 5

Industrial means technological.
Fossil fuels are fuels that are formed by the decomposition of organic material under pressure.
Abundant means available in large quantities; not scarce.
To depend on something means to need something; to rely on something.

1. A paraphrase of sentence (5) is:
    (a) Our industrial civilization depends on fossil fuels; therefore, it was started with large supplies of them. ☐
    (b) Our industrial civilization began with large supplies of fossil fuels because it now depends on them. ☐
    (c) Our industrial civilization now depends on large supplies of fossil fuels because it began with them. ☐

2. What does 'it' refer to? ....

3. What does 'them' refer to? ....

Sentence 6

Complacent means satisfied.
Renewable means able to become new again; able to be produced again in a practical period of time.

1. Why shouldn't we become complacent?

....

....

....

Sentence 7

The suffix -*less* means without. *Heed* means care.

1. What does 'heedless' mean? ....

To maintain means to keep in good condition (noun = *maintenance*).

2. A paraphrase of sentence (7) is:
   (a) We can keep our civilization in good condition without fossil fuels. ☐
   (b) If we finish our energy supplies, we will be careless about keeping our civilization in good condition. ☐
   (c) If we are not careful in our use of fossil fuels, they may soon be used up. If they are used up, we will not have enough energy to keep our civilization in good condition. ☐

Sentence 8

World-wide means throughout the world.

1. What does 'nation-wide' mean? ....

Sentence 9

1. Why are the cost of fossil fuels increasing?

   ....

Demands are strong requests; orders.

2. 'Them' refers to:
   (a) Increasing costs ☐
   (b) Fossil fuels ☐
   (c) Projects ☐

Unfeasible means not practical; not possible. *Feasible* means practical or possible. The prefix *un-* means not.

3. A paraphrase of sentence (9) is:
   (a) Because fossil fuels are so expensive, it is not often practical to use them in projects world-wide. ☐
   (b) In both developing and developed countries, it is often not possible to build projects which use fossil fuels because the demands are too high. · ☐
   (c) The demands for fossil fuels are too high and the supplies are too limited because it is often not practical to build projects which use them. ☐

39

Sentence 10

To be dependent on something means to need something.
A *dependence* is a need. (*Dependence* is the noun form of *depend*.)
To lead to means to go to (one place from another); to result in.

Sentence 11

A *situation* is a condition, a state of events.

PARAGRAPH 2
1. Which of the following *best* summarizes paragraph (2)?

    (a) The problems of using fossil fuels
    (b) Reasons that we depend on fossil fuels
    (c) Problems in the world today

Sentence 12

To be beyond one's reach means to not be available to a person.

Sentence 13

1. What is the root word of 'ability'? ....

To draw something is used here to mean to extract something.
Tides are movements of water caused by the gravitational pull of the moon.
Internal means inside. *External* means outside. The prefix *in-* means in. The prefix *ex-* means out.

2. *Interior* is the inside of an object. *Exterior* is the ....

Sentence 15

Wisely means with intelligence.

1. Where is the passive construction in this sentence?

    .... Is there an actor? .... What is the receiver

    of the action in this sentence? .... Change it to the active
    form using *someone*.

    ....

    ....

PARAGRAPH 3
1. Which of the following *best* summarizes paragraph (3)?
   (a) Using energy wisely
   (b) Possible solutions to the energy problem
   (c) Knowledge and ability

APPLY YOUR KNOWLEDGE *These questions are for those students who have finished the worksheet before the others in the class.*

1. Do you know of any examples of alternative energy use in your country? Large projects? Small projects? What about 'home-made' (traditional) designs? (For example, how do people heat their homes, get power to cook, etc.?) Write about these projects.
2. What have you read about alternative energy? Do you think it is a practical idea? Why or why not?

Review questions for discussion
1. What is one way to judge how advanced a civilization is?
2. What are some disadvantages of using fossil fuels?
3. What are some alternative energy sources? Which do you think would be best in your country? Why?

Vocabulary

Fill in the blanks or replace the words in italics using words from the vocabulary.

1. The discovery of the wheel was a .... in the history of technology.

2. Building a hydroelectric plant in a desert is not a .... idea.

3. Because of our .... use of fossil fuels, we are in danger of exhausting our supply.

4. Engineers must learn to use the earth's .... (such as the sun, wind, fossil fuels, water, etc.) economically and practically.

5. Energy from the sun is .... It arrives in huge quantities.

6. *Coal, oil and natural gas* are formed by the decomposition of

   organic material under pressure. ....

7. It takes hundreds of thousands of years to form fossil fuels. Once they are used up we cannot expect to create more in a short length of time. Fossil fuels are not *easy to produce again and*

   again. ....

8. Engineers must learn to *extract* energy from the sun, wind, and water and provide it in useful forms when and where it is

   needed most. ....

9. The whole world *needs* fossil fuels which are supplied by a limited

   number of countries. ....

10. We should not be *too satisfied* with our present day technology. This technology will be less useful as our fossil fuel supply

    decreases and gets more expensive. ....

Grammar—writing outlines

An *outline* is a summary of the main ideas in a reading or a lecture. When you take notes, you are writing a rough outline. An outline is useful for many reasons:

1. It reduces a paragraph or lecture to its most important ideas. It cuts away all the extra information.
2. It organizes the ideas of a paragraph or lecture from the general ideas to the less general ideas.
3. It organizes the ideas of a paragraph or lecture into groups according to the subject matter. (It classifies the information.)

In these ways, an outline allows you to see at a glance what the important points in a lecture or paragraph are and how they can be grouped so that you can remember them easily.

Look at the reading on alternative energy (Reading (4)). How many paragraphs are there? .... In every paragraph there is always a main idea. The main idea is the central idea of the paragraph. All of the remaining information in the paragraph relates to the main idea.

On your worksheet, you chose an idea which best summarized each paragraph. They were:

Paragraph 1: Tracing the development of civilization through the discovery and use of new energy sources
Paragraph 2: The problems of using fossil fuels
Paragraph 3: Solutions to the problems

These are, therefore, the three *main ideas* of the story about alternative energy. They are the most general ideas of the story.

An outline is written in a special form. The most general ideas are numbered with roman numerals (I, II, III, IV, etc.). We start writing them at the furthest point on the left-hand side of the page. A very general outline for the story about alternative energy is:

I Tracing the development of civilization through the discovery and use of new energy sources
II Problems of using fossil fuels
III Solutions to the problems

This outline contains no details. If we want to write a more specific outline, we must add some details. In paragraph (1) (Tracing the development of civilization through the discovery and use of new energy sources), what are the details or extra pieces of information about the main idea? In sentence (2), we find five *examples* of the discovery and use of energy. We write them out like this:

I Tracing the development of civilization through the discovery and use of new energy sources:
  A The discovery of fire
  B The domestication of animals
  C The development of agriculture
  D The invention of the steam engine
  E The use of coal and oil.

You can see that we write the second most general ideas with capital letters before them (A, B, C, D, etc.). They do not start at the far left of the page. They are written a little further to the right than the roman numerals.

An outline like the one above represents the same idea as this chart:

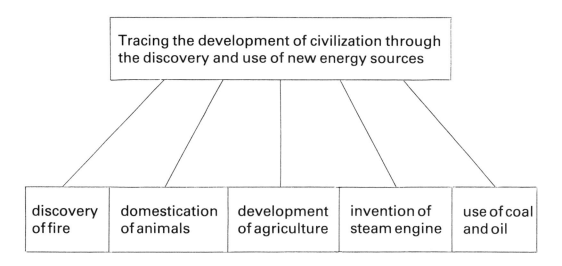

In paragraph (2) (Problems in using fossil fuels) look through the paragraph and find each problem.

II Problems in using fossil fuels:
  A Fossil fuels are not renewable.
  B Heedless use will soon exhaust our supply and leave us without the energy to maintain our civilization.
  C Increasing costs of fossil fuels make projects which use them economically unfeasible.

  D ....
     (What would you put here?)

44

If you want to add further details, we can do it by writing them further to the right, preceded by numbers (1, 2, 3, 4, etc.). They must be written directly under the heading they refer to.

Under heading C, paragraph (2), we can write the following details:

C Increasing costs of fossil fuels make projects which use them economically unfeasible.
1. Costs of fossil fuels are increasing because of limited supplies and high demands.
2. This affects both developed and developing countries.

Try to do paragraph (3).

III Possible solutions to the problem:
A Draw energy from the sun.

B ....

C ....

D ....

E ....

F ....

The complete outline is as follows:

I Tracing the development of civilization through the discovery and use of new energy sources:
A The discovery of fire
B The domestication of animals
C The development of agriculture
D The invention of the steam engine
E The use of oil and coal

II Problems in using fossil fuels:
A Fossil fuels are not renewable.
B Heedless use will exhaust our supply and leave us without the energy to maintain our civilization.
C Increasing costs of fossil fuels make projects which use them economically unfeasible.
1. Costs of fossil fuels are increasing because of limited supplies and high demands.

    2. This affects both developed and developing countries.
  D Dependence on fossil fuels leads to world-wide dependence on a limited number of countries.

III Possible solutions to the problem:
  A Draw energy from the sun.
  B Draw energy from the water.
  C Draw energy from the wind.
  D Draw energy from the tides.
  E Draw energy from the internal heat of the earth.
  F Draw energy from atoms.

The most general ideas in a paragraph should make a logical sequence and center on one common idea, i.e. the title of the story (here, alternative energy).

Also remember that each idea of the same grouping (roman numerals, capital letters, numbers, small letters) should be related and of an equal degree of generality. For example, in group II, all the capital letters are examples of problems with fossil fuels. We would not put C (1) as a capital letter because it is a detail of C and not a problem equal to the rest of the capital letters.

Exercise. *Read the following story. Then fill in the blanks in the outline.*

There are many uses for energy from the sun. The easier uses are heating water and cooking food with solar energy. Projects like these can be built with few supplies and small amounts of money. More complex (difficult) uses are heating houses and providing electricity with solar energy. Projects like these need larger amounts of money and more supplies.

I ....

  A Easy uses

    1. ....
    2. Cooking food
      (a) Project can be built with few supplies.

      (b) ....

B ....
    1. Heating homes

    2. ....

        (a) ....
        (b) Projects need large amounts of supplies.

What would a general summary of this paragraph be? (*Hint:* Look at
I (A) and I (B) for the most general ideas in the paragraph.) *Summarize
this paragraph in one short sentence.*

....

What is wrong with the following?
    A Easy uses
        1. Heating water
        2. Cooking food
        3. Project can be built with few supplies

Is (3) an easy use of solar energy? .... Is it a detail about building a

project to heat water and cook food? .... It should be like this:
    A Easy uses
        1. Heating water
        2. Cooking food
            (a) Project can be built with few supplies

Suffixes

Look at the following words from the reading: 'atom', 'atomic', 'drama', 'dramatic', 'heed', 'heedless', 'economic', 'economical', 'industry', 'industrial', 'renew', and 'renewable'. These words all have suffixes that have changed them to their adjectival forms.

Here is a list of common suffixes that form adjectives. *Fill in the blanks*:

Root	*Suffix*	*Adjective*
industry	-al	industrial (concerning industry)
....	-al	.... (concerning the nation)
to alternate	-ive	alternative (describing something that is another possibility)
to create	-ive	.... (describing something that can create)
gas	-ous	gaseous (like a gas)
poison	-ous	.... (..)
care	-ful	careful (with care)
....	-ful	beautiful (..)
heed	-less	heedless (without heed)
....	-less	.... (without a friend)
to renew	-able	renewable (able to be renewed)
to read	-able	.... (..)
gas	-like	gaslike (like a gas)
....	-like	childlike (..)

Fill in the blanks using the correct form of the root:

1. (*industr-*) Cities are often the center of ....

However, some cities are more .... than others.

2. (*creat-*) Scientists and artists must both be .... They cannot only follow old ideas. They must

.... new ones. .... is an important quality in any field.

3. (*poison*) Certain plants are .... They can kill you.

4. (*renew*) Are fossil fuels ....? 'No,' say

scientists. 'It wouldn't be easy to .... them.'

5. (*gas*) .... substances include steam, hydrogen, and oxygen.

6. (*alternat-*) An .... source of energy may be the sun.

7. (*depend, dependent, dependence, dependable*) Fossil fuels are

not very .... They aren't renewable and other countries control the supply. For this reason, we should not

be too .... on these fuels.

8. (*useful, useless, usable, use*) Fossil fuels are

.... as long as they last. When fossil fuels are exhausted, constructions which use them will no longer be

....

9. (*benefit, beneficial*) Solar energy will .... rural people in sunny areas especially. It may be

.... to the economy there, too.

10. (*agriculture*) Many developing countries have an

.... economy. The more developed they become, the more industrial they become.

49

RSFTF–C

CHAPTER 5

Vocabulary

concern	to do something indefinitely	quality
appropriate	regardless of	complex/complexity
suitable	to avoid	to operate
belief	funds	desert
to take into account	skills	costly
experts	sparsely	

Affixes

Prefix: *hydro-* (water)

Grammar

I *just as . . . so is . . .* (comparing two ideas with some similarity)

II Relative clauses

A Who

B Which

   1. Defining

   2. Non-defining

Reading 5: Appropriate technology (Part 1)

(1) Appropriate technology, which can also be called 'suitable' technology, is the name of a new area of concern for engineers. (2) Its basic beliefs are that constructions should be built taking into account the needs of the people who are using them and the materials which are available in the area. (3) Engineers should also take into account whether the constructions can be maintained indefinitely by the people who are using those constructions. (4) Right now we use power from the same fossil fuels regardless of area (environment) or economic suitability. (5) Appropriate technology tries to avoid this. (6) It also tries to avoid dependence on larger countries or large industries for funds and skills. (7) Appropriate technology tries to make constructions which are simple so that parts can be found easily and so that they can be maintained without experts. (8) Complexity does not necessarily mean quality. (9) In some cases, the machines which are the simplest to build and operate are also those that will do the most good. (10) Just as building a hydroelectric plant in a desert is unsuitable, so is building a power plant that is costly and difficult to maintain in a poor, sparsely populated area.

Worksheet

Sentence 1

A *concern* is an interest; a worry.
Appropriate means *suitable*; proper for a particular time or place.

1. 'A new area of concern for engineers' means:
   (a) Something new that engineers are worried about ☐
   (b) A new kind of interest (study) for engineers ☐
   (c) A different place where engineers can go to discuss their problems ☐

Sentences 2 and 3

A *belief* is the noun form of *to believe*.
To take into account means to consider, to think about.

1. Underline the three things that an engineer should take into account before building a construction.

2. What kind of materials should an engineer who is using appropriate technology build with?
   (a) Materials that he takes into account ☐
   (b) Materials that can be easily found in the area ☐
   (c) Materials which are modern and difficult to maintain ☐
   (d) None of the above ☐

3. In sentence (2), 'its' refers to:
   (a) A new area of concern for engineers ☐
   (b) Engineers ☐
   (c) Appropriate technology ☐
   (d) (a) and (c) ☐
   (e) None of the above ☐

4. In sentence (2), 'them' refers to:
   (a) Engineers ☐
   (b) A new area of concern ☐
   (c) Construction ☐
   (d) (a) and (c) ☐
   (e) None of the above ☐

53

5. 'To maintain something indefinitely' means:
   - (a) To not be sure about keeping something in good condition ☐
   - (b) To occasionally keep something in good condition ☐
   - (c) To keep something in good condition for as long a time as needed (the time is indefinite) ☐
   - (d) None of the above ☐

Sentence 4

Regardless of area means not considering the area.

1. 'Regardless of economic suitability' means

   ....

2. An example of building a construction regardless of area or economic suitability is:
   - (a) Building a multi-million dollar generator to supply electricity to New York City ☐
   - (b) Building a multi-million dollar generator to supply electricity to a town of 100 people located 10 hours from the nearest large city ☐
   - (c) Building a hydroelectric plant in a desert ☐
   - (d) (b) and (c) ☐
   - (e) All of the above ☐

Sentence 5

To avoid means to prevent; to try not to do something.

1. 'This' refers to:
   - (a) Using engineers ☐
   - (b) Using power from the same fossil fuels regardless of area or economic suitability ☐
   - (c) Using materials that are available in the area ☐
   - (d) (b) and (c) ☐
   - (e) None of the above ☐

Sentence 6

1. Which form of *to depend* is 'dependence'?
   - (a) Adjective ☐
   - (b) Noun ☐
   - (c) Verb ☐

Funds means the money and supplies available for something.
Skills means special knowledge and ability.

Sentence 7

Experts are people who have skills; people who have special know-ledge, training, or ability.

Sentence 8

Quality means degree of excellence.
Complex means complicated; difficult.

1. Which form of *complex* is 'complexity'?
   (a) Adjective
   (b) Noun
   (c) Verb

2. 'Complexity' means:
   (a) Difficult
   (b) Degree of difficulty
   (c) To be difficult

3. A paraphrase of sentence (8) is:
   (a) The difficulty of a construction is not always a measure of how good it is.
   (b) It is not necessary for something to be complex in order to have a high degree of quality.
   (c) Being difficult is not always good.
   (d) All of the above

Sentence 9

To operate something means to make something work.

1. 'Those' refers to:
   (a) Machines
   (b) Experts
   (c) Complexity
   (d) None of the above

Sentence 10

Hydro- is a prefix meaning water. A *hydroelectric plant* is a construction that provides electricity which is powered by water.
A *desert* is a very dry, usually sandy area.
Sparsely means spread out, not concentrated.
Costly means expensive.

1. Rural areas are sparsely populated; in contrast, ... areas are not.
2. A sentence with *just as . . . so is . . .* is a sentence where two ideas are compared and have some similarity. In sentence (9), a hydro-electric plant in a desert and an expensive power plant that is difficult to maintain for a poor, sparsely populated area are compared and related by the idea that:
   (a) They are both unsuitable ☐
   (b) They are both inappropriate ☐
   (c) One is unsuitable; the other is not ☐
   (d) (a) and (b) ☐
   (e) None of the above ☐

APPLY YOUR KNOWLEDGE *This question is for those students who have finished the worksheet before others in the class.*

Choose two different areas in your country. You are going to look at each area as if you were an engineer there trying to use appropriate technology. Make a list of the people's energy needs for that area. (For example, what do they need energy for? How much energy?) Consider where the area is. Is it practical to have experts maintain it? Consider the economy of the area. Is the area sparsely populated or not? What kind of energy would you consider for them?

Outline

Fill in the 5 basic beliefs of appropriate technology.

I Basic beliefs of appropriate technology:

A ....

B ....

C ....
D Tries to avoid using fuels regardless of area or economic suit-
   ability.
   1. Right now, we use fossil fuels regardless of area or economic
      suitability

E ....

F ....
   1. So that parts can be found easily
   2. So that constructions can be maintained without experts
   3. Complexity doesn't necessarily mean quality.
      (a) A hydroelectric plant in a desert is unsuitable.
      (b) A power plant that is costly and difficult to maintain, in a
          poor, sparsely populated area, is unsuitable.

Vocabulary

Fill in the blanks with words from the vocabulary.

1. Everyone is equal .... of the family they come from. Their family should not be considered when judging a person.

2. Machines often break down because people don't know how to

   .... them.

3. If something is suitable for its area, its job, and population, it is

   said to be ....

4. In many complex constructions, we need .... to maintain the machines because the average person does not have the special knowledge and skills that are needed to do it himself.

5. When a scientist tries to make a theory, he must first

   .... all the possible hypotheses. He should consider every possibility.

6. Scientists no longer have the .... that fossil fuels are our only energy supply.

7. The .... of an engineer include the ability to design and draw plans for machines.

8. If a construction is .... to operate and maintain, it is not appropriate for a poor area.

9. New York City is not .... populated; in fact, it is quite crowded.

10. The .... of the materials was poor. That is why the construction started breaking down within two years.

Grammar—relative clauses

Look at sentence (1) in the reading. This sentence is made up of two sentences which share the same subject.

1. Appropriate technology is the name of a new area of concern for engineers.
2. Appropriate technology can also be called 'suitable' technology.

We can combine two sentences with the same subject or object by forming sentences with relative clauses. To do this, we:

(a) See which words the two sentences have in common (subject or object).

(b) Insert the second sentence into the first sentence immediately following the common word(s).

(c) Replace the repeating word(s) in the relative clause with *which* or *that* if it refers to a non-human or inanimate (not living) thing. If it is a person, use *who*. This relative pronoun is always at the beginning of the relative clause.

Look at the two sentences above again.

Step (a) *We see that the common subject is* 'appropriate technology'.

Step (b) *We insert sentence 2 inside sentence 1 after* 'appropriate technology':
Appropriate technology, appropriate technology can also be called 'suitable' technology, is the name of a new area of concern for engineers.

Step (c) *We replace* 'appropriate technology' *(the repeating words) in sentence (2) with* which *because it is inanimate:*
Appropriate technology, *which* can also be called 'suitable' technology, is the name of a new area of concern for engineers.

Notice that in this sentence, the relative clause ('which can also be called "suitable" technology') gives us *extra* informationabout the subject. The sentence is still understandable and logical if we remove the relative clause. The meaning of the sentence is not changed if we remove the relative clause. ('Appropriate technology is the name of a new area of concern for engineers.') This kind of relative clause is called a *non-defining relative clause*.

Non-defining relative clauses are separated from the first sentence by commas which show that the clause is not necessary because it only gives *extra* information. It can be removed without changing the desired meaning of a sentence.

Look at sentence (8) in the reading: 'In some cases, the machines which are the simplest to build and operate are also those that will do the most good.' The two sentences contained in sentence (8) are:

1. In most cases, the machines are also those that will do the most good.

2. The machines are the simplest to build and operate.

What words are common to both sentences? .... Therefore, we insert the second sentence after 'the machines' in sentence (1) because the second sentence refers to those machines. We replace 'the machines' in the relative clause with *which* because machines are inanimate.

Notice that sentence (2) does not give extra information about the machines. It gives *necessary* information. It tells us *which kind* of machines we are talking about. It *limits* the group of machines we are referring to. We are not talking about all machines in sentence (8); we are only referring to machines 'which are simplest to build and operate'. If we remove the relative clause, the sentence loses its desired meaning. This type of relative clause is called a *defining relative clause* because it tells us what kind of thing we are referring to or limits the general group. It is not surrounded by commas because it is not optional and is necessary to keep the meaning of the sentence.

Sometimes the meaning depends on whether the sentence is defining or non-defining. For example:

Non-defining: My uncle, who is a teacher, visited me last week.

Can you tell from this sentence if I have more than one uncle?

If so, how can you tell? ....

....

Defining: My uncle who is a teacher visited me last week.

Can you tell from this sentence if I have more than one uncle?

If so, how can you tell? ....

....

In the sentence with the defining clause, the relative clause 'who is a teacher' is telling us which uncle we are referring to (i.e., this is the uncle who is a teacher, not the uncle who is a doctor). There must be more than one uncle. The non-defining clause just gives extra information. I may have one or many uncles. You cannot tell in that sentence.

Exercises

Indicate the sentence which is a combination of the sentences given. For example:

Hydrogen is a light gas.
Hydrogen has only one proton and one electron.
(a) Hydrogen which has only one proton and one electron is a light gas. ☐
(b) Hydrogen, which has only one proton and one electron, is a light gas. ☐
(c) Hydrogen has only one proton and one electron which is a light gas. ☐
(d) None of the above. ☐

Since the repeating word is 'hydrogen', the relative clause must follow 'hydrogen'. Sentence (c) is therefore incorrect. The difference between (a) and (b) is that (a) is defining and (b) is non-defining. Does the relative clause tell us what kind of hydrogen we are talking about? No. All hydrogen has one proton and one electron. Therefore, the relative clause only gives us extra information. It is non-defining; (b) is the correct answer.

1. Hydrogen is a light gas.
   This hydrogen has two neutrons.
   (a) Hydrogen, which has two neutrons, is a light gas. ☐
   (b) Hydrogen which has two neutrons is a light gas. ☐
   (c) Hydrogen has two neutrons which is a light gas. ☐
   (d) None of the above. ☐

(*Hint:* The number of neutrons in hydrogen may change.)

2. The country needs engineers.
   The engineers have experience.
   (a) The country needs engineers who have experience. ☐
   (b) The country needs engineers which have experience. ☐
   (c) The country which has experience needs engineers. ☐
   (d) None of the above. ☐

3. The countries need engineers.
   The countries are developing.
   (a) The countries need engineers who are developing. ☐

(b) The countries are developing which need engineers. ☐
(c) The countries which are developing need engineers. ☐

What is the difference between these two sentences?
'The countries which are developing need engineers'
'The countries, which are developing, need engineers'

....

....

4. Windmills are examples of using alternative energy sources to
   provide power.
   Windmills were invented in Iran.
   (a) Windmills which were invented in Iran are examples of
       using alternative energy sources to provide power. ☐
   (b) Windmills were invented in Iran which are examples of
       using alternative energy sources to provide power. ☐
   (c) Windmills, which were invented in Iran, are examples of
       using alternative energy sources to provide power. ☐
   (d) None of the above. ☐

*Indicate the sentences which make up the given sentences in numbers
(5)–(8).*

5. Complexity, which does not necessarily mean quality, is avoided
   by engineers who use appropriate technology.
   (a) Complexity does not necessarily mean quality.
       Quality is avoided by some engineers.
       These engineers use appropriate technology. ☐
   (b) Complexity does not necessarily mean quality.
       Complexity is avoided by all engineers.
       All engineers use appropriate technology. ☐
   (c) Complexity does not necessarily mean quality.
       Complexity is avoided by some engineers.
       These engineers use appropriate technology. ☐
   (d) None of the above. ☐

6. Atomic energy, which may be more dangerous than helpful, uses
   materials which are radioactive.
   (a) Atomic energy may be more dangerous than helpful.
       Atomic energy uses all materials.
       All materials are radioactive. ☐

(b) Atomic energy may be more dangerous than helpful.
Atomic energy uses some materials.
These materials are radioactive. ☐

(c) Atomic energy is radioactive.
Atomic energy uses all materials.
All materials may be more dangerous than helpful ☐

(d) None of the above. ☐

7. Afghanistan, which has a population of approximately 16,000,000 people who are almost all Moslem, could use sunlight as an alternative source of energy.

(a) Afghanistan could use sunlight as an alternative source of energy. There are almost 16,000,000 Moslems in the world. Almost all Moslems could use sunlight from Afghanistan. ☐

(b) Afghanistan has a population of approximately 16,000,000 people. 16,000,000 people are Moslem. Moslems could use sunlight as an alternative source of energy. ☐

(c) Afghanistan could use sunlight as an alternative source of energy. Afghanistan has a population of approximately 16,000,000. These 16,000,000 are almost all Moslem. ☐

(d) None of the above. ☐

8. Students who use this book and who study hard will improve their reading comprehension and vocabulary skills.

(a) All students will improve their reading comprehension and vocabulary skills. All students use this book. All students study hard. ☐

(b) Some students will improve their reading comprehension and vocabulary skills. These students use this book. These students study hard. ☐

(c) All students use this book. Some students study hard. Some students will improve their reading comprehension and vocabulary skills. ☐

(d) None of the above. ☐

CHAPTER 6

Vocabulary

to be concerned with something		to cut down on something
to upset	native	waste products
balance	instead of	pollution/to pollute
interrelationship	in the long run	to pose a threat
organisms	to be within reach	to be aware of something
environment	efficiency	

Affixes

I Prefix *dis-* — not

II Prefix *inter* — between

Grammar

I Using context clues

II Changing adjectives and nouns to verb phrases

    A *to be* + adjective + preposition

    B *to have* + noun + preposition

Reading 6: Appropriate technology (Part 2)

(1) Appropriate technology is concerned with not upsetting the balance of the earth's forces. (2) The science which studies this balance and the interrelationships between organisms and their environments is called ecology. (3) One way of not upsetting this balance is by using native materials instead of bringing in foreign elements. (4) Try to use what is available in the area. (5) In the long run, these materials will always be within reach. (6) They will also probably be the cheapest materials which are available in the area. (7) In a desert, use sun power. (8) In a rain forest, use water power. (9) Other ways of not upsetting the balance in an environment are to increase the efficiency of constructions and to cut down on unusable waste products. (10) Already, in many parts of the world, air and water pollution pose a threat to human life. (11) Engineers must be aware of the dangers of pollution.

Worksheet

Sentence 1

To upset means to put into disorder (*dis-* = not, + order = not in order); to disturb an arrangement.
A *balance* is a proper arrangement of things.
To upset the balance is to make an arrangement out of proportion or out of order; to cause an imbalance.

1. Which of the following is an example of 'upsetting the balance of the earth's forces'?

   (a) All the trees were cut down in a mountainous area of Greece. Because the trees no longer held the soil together, erosion (the wearing down of something by rain, wind, sun, etc.) increased. Animals died because they no longer had food or protection. ☐

   (b) A chemical plant was built in Italy. Chemicals escaped without being noticed. Animals died. People had to leave their homes indefinitely because the land was no longer good for growing things. ☐

   (c) All the wastes from a village were thrown in the river. The fish died. The water became undrinkable. ☐

   (d) All of the above. ☐

   (e) None of the above. ☐

Sentence 2

An *interrelationship* is a giving and taking relationship between two or more things (*inter-* = between).
Organisms are all living things.
The *environment* means the surroundings and everything in the surroundings.

1. The two sentences which make up sentence (2) are:

   (a) All science studies this balance and the interrelationship of organisms and their environments. All science is called ecology. ☐

   (b) The science is called ecology. This science studies this balance and the interrelationship of organisms and their environments. ☐

   (c) This balance and the interrelationship of organisms and their environments studies science. This science is called ecology. ☐
   (d) None of the above. ☐

2. Organisms include (indicate as many as are correct):
   (a) Students ☐
   (b) Animals ☐
   (c) Rocks ☐
   (d) Plants ☐

Sentence 3

Something that is *native* to an area is found in that area.
Instead of means in place of.

1. A paraphrase of sentence (3) is:
   (a) Using native elements and bringing in foreign elements won't change the environment in an area. ☐
   (b) Using materials that are found in the area of the construction may be better than using materials that must be brought from places outside the area. It may be better because it won't change the environment. ☐
   (c) Using foreign elements is better than using materials that are found locally (in the same area) because they might upset the environment. ☐
   (d) None of the above. ☐

Sentence 5

In the long run means over the years; through time.
To be within reach means to be available; to be possible.

1. 'These materials' refers to:
   (a) Materials which are foreign ☐
   (b) Materials which are available in the area ☐
   (c) Native materials ☐
   (d) (b) and (c) ☐
   (e) All of the above ☐

Sentence 6

1. Using native materials is good because:
   (a) They will be cheapest for the area ☐
   (b) They will always be available ☐
   (c) They will not upset the balance of the earth's forces ☐

(d) (b) and (c)

(e) All of the above

Sentence 9

Efficiency is the best possible use of power and materials without waste.

To cut down on something means to reduce the amount of something.

Waste products are garbage or any material that cannot be used any longer by a construction or system.

Sentence 10

Pollution is the state of being dirty; impure. The verb form is *to pollute.*

To pose a threat means to be a danger.

1. All the wastes from a village were thrown in a river. The fish died. The water became undrinkable. This is an example of pollution of the:

(a) Air

(b) Water

(c) Land

(d) (a) and (b)

Sentence 11

To be aware of something means to be concerned with something; to notice something.

Complete the outline:

Appropriate technology

I Tries to avoid upsetting the balance of the earth's forces (ecology)

A ....

1. Because these materials will always be within reach
2. Because they will probably always be the cheapest materials for the area

(a) ....

(b) ....

B ....

C ....

1. In many parts of the world, air and water pollution are a danger to human life.
2. Engineers must be aware of the dangers of pollution.

| APPLY YOUR KNOWLEDGE | *This exercise is for those students who have finished the worksheet before the others in the class.*

Referring to the beliefs of appropriate technology listed in this reading and the last reading, explain why the following situation is *not* an example of appropriate technology.

    In a town of 100 people the government wants to build an electric power plant. It is a rural area and the people only need small supplies of electricity. The government has made an agreement to receive funds from international organizations in the form of a long-term loan. It is a new design and so they are bringing in experts from America, Russia, and China. The plant will be powered by oil. The country does not produce oil. The waste products from the plant will go into the nearby river.

....

....

....

....

....

Vocabulary

Fill in the blanks using words from the vocabulary.

1. Oil is .... to Saudi Arabia. It is found there.

2. People often think about what is best for the present. They must

   also think about what is best ....

3. .... is caused by allowing waste products to mix with our
   air and water.

4. Everyone should .... with the danger of exhausting our
   supply of fossil fuels. Everyone is affected by it.

5. *Unusable wastes* in the air *are a danger* to all organisms.

   ....; ....

6. Introducing foreign materials into an area can *disturb* the special

   balance of forces in the area. ....

7. A company increased the .... of their constructions and
   found that it cost more at the beginning but cost less in the long
   run.

8. We should be looking for alternatives to fossil fuels ....
   looking for more ways to use them.

9. .... is concerned with the relationship between
   organisms and the environment.

Grammar

Many verb phrases have the form: *to be* + adjective + preposition.
Examples in the paragraph are 'be concerned with' and 'be aware of'.
This is one way to form a verb phrase from an adjective.

Other verb phrases have the form: *to have* + noun + preposition.
This is one way to form a verb phrase from a noun.

Adjective	*Noun*	*Verb phrase*
concerned	—	be concerned with $\left\{\begin{array}{l}\text{something}\\\text{verb} + ing\\\text{someone}\end{array}\right\}$ be concerned about Appropriate technology is concerned with conservation. (It is interested in conservation.) Engineers are concerned about exhausting our energy supply. (They are worried about exhausting our energy supply.)
aware	awareness	be aware of $\left\{\begin{array}{l}\text{something}\\\text{verb} + ing\end{array}\right\}$ have an awareness of $\left\{\begin{array}{l}\text{something}\\\text{verb} + ing\end{array}\right\}$
certain	certainty	be certain $\left\{\begin{array}{l}\text{of}\\\text{about}\end{array}\right\}$ $\left\{\begin{array}{l}\text{something}\\\text{verb} + ing\end{array}\right\}$ have a certainty about $\left\{\begin{array}{l}\text{something}\\\text{verb} + ing\end{array}\right\}$
sure	—	be sure of $\left\{\begin{array}{l}\text{something}\\\text{verb} + ing\end{array}\right\}$
different	—	be different from $\left\{\begin{array}{l}\text{something}\\\text{verb} + ing\end{array}\right\}$
familiar	familiarity	be familiar with $\left\{\begin{array}{l}\text{something}\\\text{verb} + ing\end{array}\right\}$ have a familiarity with $\left\{\begin{array}{l}\text{something}\\\text{verb} + ing\end{array}\right\}$

interested	interest	be interested in $\begin{cases} \text{something} \\ \text{verb} + ing \end{cases}$
		have an interest in $\begin{cases} \text{something} \\ \text{verb} + ing \end{cases}$
known	knowledge	be known for $\begin{cases} \text{something} \\ \text{verb} + ing \end{cases}$
		have a knowledge of $\begin{cases} \text{something} \\ \text{verb} + ing \end{cases}$

Newton is known for his law of gravity.
Newton is known for discovering the law of gravity. (Newton is famous because he discovered the law of gravity.)

He has a knowledge of the law of gravity. (He knows about and understands the law of gravity.)

Fill in the blanks with a form of the word in parentheses.

1. (*aware*) He .... the dangers of exhausting our fossil fuel supply.

2. (*familiar*) .... you

.... the beliefs of appropriate technology?

3. (*known*) France .... its excellent wine.

4. (*different*) Learning to read English .... learning to speak English.

5. (*interest*) They .... all new ideas in the field of medicine.

6. (*concerned*) Families .... not having enough wood to heat their houses this winter.

7. (*concerned*) Engineers .... new ideas in technology.

8. (*not sure*) They .... receiving enough fuel for next winter.

9. (*different*) Fossil fuels .... energy from the sun in that solar power is renewable but fossil fuels aren't.

10. (*knowledge*) It is not necessary to .... engineering to understand the ideas of appropriate technology.

Using context clues

Often when students read books in a foreign language, they find words they don't know. If they have a lot of time (and patience!), they look up all the words in a dictionary. Frequently, however, a student doesn't have the time or doesn't want to interrupt his reading. These are the times that skills in using *context clues* are useful.

A *clue* is something that helps a person solve (answer) a problem; a hint. Clues to the meaning of a word may be found in the rest of the sentence.

A *context* is what comes before and after a word. If a student does not know a word, he looks at the context clues. He thinks back to what he was reading before he came to the unknown word. He reads ahead to see what will happen after the unknown word.

Context clues are hints from the rest of the sentence or story that in various ways help a student understand the meaning of an unknown word.

1. Some context clues are found in sentences which repeat the same information. For example:

   The computer is *infallible*. It never makes a mistake.

2. Sometimes the definition can be found in the same sentence. For example:

   Context clues can *clarify* unknown words and make their meanings clearer.

3. Some sentences contain words such as *but, however* and *nevertheless*. These words tell you that the following information will *contrast* or be the opposite of the information that comes before it. For example:

   Solar energy may *supplement* other sources of energy; however, it can never replace them totally.

Some engineers don't think that we can extract any energy from the sun. They *underestimate* the possible use of solar energy. However, other engineers think that we can get all of our energy from the sun. They *overestimate* the possible use of solar power.

4. Lastly, in some sentences, the meaning of words can be found through the use of logic. The meaning is not stated but there is enough information to give you an idea of the meaning. For example:

You couldn't stay in the sun for more than five minutes yesterday because the heat was so *intense*.

Read the following sentences. Using context clues, write out a definition of the underlined words. Do not use a dictionary.

1. The teacher listened to the *queries* of the students and answered them.

   ....

2. If a construction is not *sturdy*, we cannot expect it to last a long time.

   ....

3. Cigarette smoking may be *detrimental* to your health.

   ....

4. The price of oil is becoming *exorbitant*; however, solar energy will always be free.

   ....

5. The amount of usable solar energy *diminishes* as the days get shorter.

   ....

6. When people first saw electricity, they were *astonished*. They were so surprised, they couldn't believe their eyes.

   ....

7. Pollution is often a *conglomeration*, or mixture, of chemicals.

   ....

8. The *mortality rate* for children in developing countries is higher than in developed countries. Many children die before the age of five.

   ....

9. Engineers should *take the initiative* themselves to use alternative energy sources. They should not wait to see if other people will use it first.

   ....

10. Gears are *integral* parts of wind-powered generators; they are absolutely necessary.

   ....

Notes:

CHAPTER 7

Reading 7: Introduction to solar energy: the sun as a source of energy

(1) Most of the energy we consume comes directly or indirectly from the sun. (2) In 1972, man consumed 90 trillion horsepower hours of energy. (3) During the same year, the sun emitted 1.5 million trillion horsepower hours of sunlight on the planet. (4) Only a small fraction of this natural force (40 billion kilowatts) is converted by green plants into all the food and timber that grows on the earth. (5) Over hundreds of thousands of years this vegetation is eventually converted into fossil fuels like coal and oil. (6) Because of the time which is required to produce fossil fuels, it would be more feasible to employ solar radiations directly to help meet out energy needs. (7) Presently, solar energy can be used to stretch our finite supplies of fossil fuels. (8) Experiments have already shown that we can heat a house, heat water, air condition buildings, cook food, and produce electricity with solar energy. (9) Scientists have even converted an automobile to run on batteries which are charged by solar cells. (10) In the future, solar energy may be one of our main sources of energy.

Worksheet

Sentence 1

1. Here are dictionary definitions for *to consume*. They are all correct; however, in sentence (1) 'to consume' has only one of these meanings. Which definition *best* fits the meaning of 'consume' in sentence (1)? *Check the number.*

   con·sume – vb – 1. to do away with completely; to destroy ☐
   2. to eat or drink; especially in great quantity ☐
   3. to use up ☐

2. We use power from the sun. We use solar power. *Solar* is the

   .... form which means relating to the sun or operated by the sun.
   (a) Noun ☐
   (b) Verb ☐
   (c) Adjective ☐

Sentence 2

Horsepower hours means the work performed or energy consumed by working at the rate of one horsepower (a unit of power equal to 746 watts) for one hour.

Sentence 3

1. 'During the same year' refers to .... (What year?)

2. Using context clues, what could 'emit' mean? ....

Sentence 4

1. 'This natural force' refers to:
   (a) The 90 trillion horsepower hours of energy consumed by man. ☐
   (b) The 1.5 million trillion horsepower hours of sunlight. ☐
   (c) The natural force of green plants. ☐
   (d) None of the above.

To convert means to change from one form to another. The noun form is *conversion.*
Timber means growing trees or their wood.

RSFTF–D

Sentence 5

Vegetation includes all plant life.

1. Look at sentences (4) and (5). Can you fill in the blanks with information from the sentences?

.... convert .... into

.... Then .... is converted into

....

Sentence 6

Solar radiation is energy from the sun sent out in the form of waves or particles.

1. Which of the following is a paraphrase of sentence (6)?
   (a) It would be most practical if we could get some solar energy directly to meet our energy needs because we require so much time to produce fossil fuels. ☐
   (b) It would be most practical if we could get some solar energy directly to meet our energy needs; therefore, we require so much time to produce fossil fuels. ☐
   (c) We require so much time to produce fossil fuels; therefore, it would be most practical if we could get some solar energy directly to help meet our energy needs. ☐
   (d) (a) and (c). ☐
   (e) None of the above. ☐

Sentence 7

Finite means having definite or definable limits. It is the opposite of *infinite*.

1. Here is a dictionary definition of *to stretch*. All of the meanings are correct but only one of them fits the meaning of *to stretch* in sentence (7). *Check that number.*

   stretch – vb – 1. to extend in length ☐
   2. to lie down at full length ☐
   3. to extend over a continuous period ☐

2. How can solar energy stretch our supplies of fossil fuels?
   (a) Solar energy can convert green plants to fossil fuels more quickly. ☐

(b) It can be used at the same time as fossil fuels. It will supplement (be in addition to) our supplies of fossil fuels. ☐

(c) It can make our supplies of fossil fuels grow — for example, from New York to Cairo. ☐

Sentence 9

1. The two sentences that make up sentence (9) are:
   (a) Scientists have even converted an automobile to run on all batteries. All batteries are charged by solar cells. ☐
   (b) Scientists have even converted an automobile to run on batteries. Solar cells charge these batteries. ☐
   (c) Scientists have even converted an automobile to run on batteries. These batteries are charged by solar cells. ☐
   (d) (b) and (c). ☐
   (e) None of the above. ☐

| APPLY YOUR KNOWLEDGE | *These exercises are for those students who have finished the worksheet before others in the class.*

1. Write a paragraph about the difficulties you think engineers could have when using solar energy.

....

....

....

....

....

....

....

....

....

....

Now ?

2. Write a paragraph about this cartoon.

....

....

....

....

....

Outline

Two students were asked to summarize reading (7). One said, 'This paragraph tells us about the indirect use of solar energy. Then it tells us about the direct use of solar energy.' The other student said, 'No! This paragraph tells us about the use of solar power through time. It starts in the past, goes to the present, and finishes in the future.'

The teacher asked, 'Well, who's right? We know that a correct summarizing idea can be used as the heading of an outline. Let's try to make an outline of the paragraph about solar energy using the heading *Direct and indirect uses of solar energy*.

I Direct and indirect uses of solar energy:

  A ....

     1. The sun emits 1.5 million trillion horsepower hours of sunlight.

     2. ....

     3. ....

     4. Man uses fossil fuels, vegetation, and timber.

  B ....

     1. Used to stretch our finite supplies of fossil fuels.

       (a) ....

       (b) Heat water

       (c) ....

       (d) ....

       (e) ....

       (f) ....

'Not bad! That summarizes the paragraph pretty well. How about trying *The use of solar energy through time* as a heading now?'

I The use of solar energy through time:
  A The past

      1. ....

      2. ....

      3. Only a small fraction of this natural force is converted by green plants into all the food and timber that grow on the earth.

      4. ....

  B ....

      1. Solar energy can be used to stretch our finite supplies of fossil fuels.

        (a) ....

        (b) Heat water

        (c) ....

        (d) ....

        (e) ....

        (f) ....

  C The future
      1. Solar power may be one of our main sources of energy.

'That's O.K. too. Can we have two good outlines for one paragraph? Yes. Each outline directs our attention to what the student thought were the most important ideas of the paragraph. Sometimes the student decides what is most important. The first student thought that the direct and indirect uses of solar energy were the central ideas of the paragraph. The second student thought that the use of solar energy through time (from the past to the future) was the central idea. Both are right. A paragraph is *interpreted* by the student who reads it. Each one decided what is important and what should be remembered.'

The second student arranged the ideas in the paragraph according to a *time sequence*. Many paragraphs are arranged into time sequences, i.e. logical orders of time. This is called *chronological order*.

A paragraph is a group of sentences developing one idea. In most paragraphs, there is a sentence that states the main idea. It introduces the rest of the paragraph. This sentence is called the *topic sentence*. It is often, but not always, the first or second sentence.

Exercises

In each of the following groups of sentences, one sentence is a possible topic sentence. The rest of the sentences are details about the topic sentence. In this exercise, they are details that can be arranged in chronological order. *Rearrange the sentences in each group to form a logical paragraph*. The words in italics will give you clues about the sequence of events. Write *1* next to the topic sentence, *2* next to the next sentence, *3* next to the third sentence, and so on.

Group 1

.... Cloth with a wooden frame has been used for hundreds of centuries for converting the useful energy of the wind into mechanical work, especially grinding grain and pumping water.

.... *Within 100 years*, the use of windmills spread to China.

.... *Now, thirteen centuries later*, we are again realizing the possibilities of using wind power.

.... *There*, in China, the art of sailmaking (*sails* – the pieces of cloth on the frames) was greatly improved.

.... The use of windmills began in Iran *in the seventh century*.

Group 2

.... In *this* way, the wind produces a rotating motion.

.... *Next*, the power from the rotating motion is increased by using gears.

.... The wind *first* comes and catches on the blades of the mill.

87

.... *Finally,* this power is used to grind the wheat.

.... A windmill is a simple machine for grinding wheat.

Group 3

.... *To begin with,* the sides of our collector box were built.

.... Collector boxes are essential parts of solar heating projects and should be built carefully.

.... *In the third place,* aluminum foil was cemented to the back piece of wood so that it could act as a reflector.

.... *In the second place,* a groove was cut in each side to hold glass.

.... *Subsequently (next),* copper tubing was bent into a series of S-turns and made to lie as close as possible to *this* sheet copper.

.... *In the fourth place,* five small cubes were nailed to the back piece of wood to hold the sheet copper.

.... *Then* the copper tubing was soldered to the sheet copper.

.... *Lastly,* the base was fixed to the sides with the glass in place.

Group 4

.... *During those* years of both working and studying, *he* didn't have much time to sleep.

.... Mohammed Gul is *presently* a student at the university.

.... *After* graduating from the university, approximately three years from now, *he* wants to work on an engineering project near his home town.

.... *Prior to* studying at the university, *he* had gone to high school and worked on his father's farm *simultaneously.*

As you can see, there are many vocabulary words that make time sequences clearer. Some are:

> before = earlier = prior to
> formerly = previously
> during = while = at the same time = while simultaneously
> around (*length of time*) ago = approximately (*length of time*) ago
> between (*time, event*) and (*time, event*)
> in (*year*)
> on (*day*)
> since (*time, event*)
> after = later
> now = nowadays = presently
> to begin with = in the first place = first of all
> next = then = subsequently = in the next place
> at last = in conclusion = finally = lastly

Prefixes

The opposite of *finite* is *infinite*. The prefix *in-* means not. What is the opposite of *appropriate*? .... *efficient*? ....

combustible? .... *soluble*? .... *sufficient*?

....

The prefix *in-* changes, however, depending on the letter that follows it. For example, the prefix is *ir-* when the first letter of the root word is an *r*. The opposite of *replaceable* is *irreplaceable*. What is the

opposite of *rational*? ....

The prefix is *il-* when the first letter of the root word is an *l*. An example is *logical* and *illogical*. What is the opposite of *legal*?

....

The prefix is *im-* when the first letter of the root word is *m*, *p*, or *b*. The opposite of *probable* is *improbable*. What is the opposite of

practical? .... *moderate*? .... *balance* (noun)?

....

Therefore, *in-*, *ir-*, *il-*, and *im-* all mean not, but change according to the letter following them.
Write the opposite of the following words:

flexible ....   measurable ....

patient ....   adequate ....

movable ....   permanent ....

direct ....   perfect ....

constant ....   variable ....

Other prefixes that change the root word to its opposite are:

un-   unable, unnecessary, unreasonable

dis-   disuse (noun), disproportional, disorder

non-   non-metal, nonsense, non-defining clause

Solar water heaters at Bemabo, Mali

CHAPTER 8

Vocabulary

to employ	matte paint	to extend
version	hose	tank
to install	groove	to circulate
permanent	to reflect	latter
" = inch, inches	to bend	former
' = foot, feet	series	to be made of
cut to size	to solder	to consist of
valve	to assemble	to contain
fitting	in place	to be filled with

Grammar

I Using chronological order to read directions

II Describing functions (uses)

  A *may be used to*

  B *may be used for*

  C *may be used as a means of*

Skills

I Reading diagrams

We have seen how chronological order is used in paragraphs. Chronological order is also used when writing *directions* for doing or building something. However, since directions are numbered, it is not necessary to use special vocabulary like *first, next, subsequently*, etc.

Reading 8: Building a solar water heater

There are many solar water heaters presently in use, and we can expect to employ the sun as a water heater often in the future. The water heater described here has a capacity of only five gallons. However, an enlarged version of this heater could be installed on a roof, connected to a water supply, and used as a permanent source of hot water.

Materials
1″ × 4″ board (8 ft.)
$\frac{1}{2}$″ plywood (one piece 24″ × 24″)
single weight window glass (one piece cut to size)
$\frac{3}{8}$″ copper tubing (approximately 16 ft.)
sheet copper (22″ × 22″)
$\frac{1}{2}$″ valve
$\frac{3}{4}$″ hose fitting
$\frac{3}{8}$″ plastic hose (10 ft.)
$\frac{1}{4}$ × 1$\frac{1}{2}$″ wood screws (approximately 30)
$\frac{1}{2}$″ copper tubing (3″)
five-gallon can
matte black paint

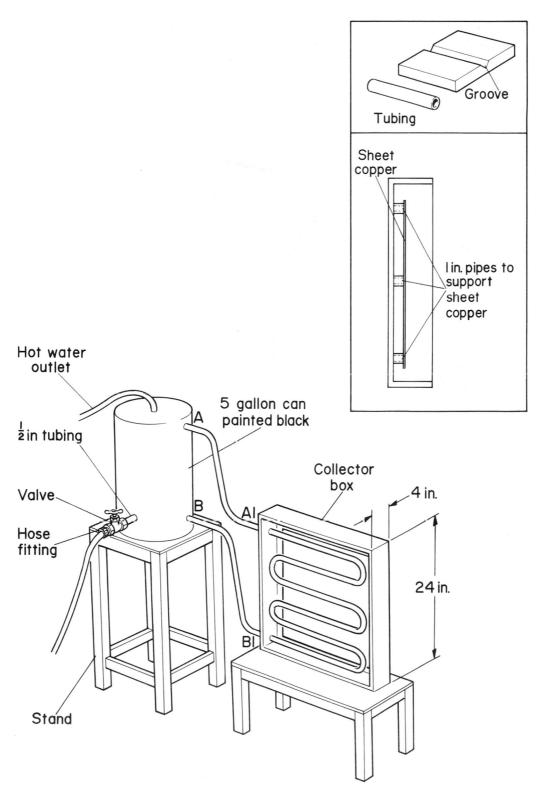

Groove

Tubing

Sheet copper

l in. pipes to support sheet copper

Hot water outlet

$\frac{1}{2}$ in tubing

Valve

Hose fitting

Stand

5 gallon can painted black

A

B

Al

Collector box

4 in.

24 in.

Bl

Directions for construction

1. Build the sides of the collector box from 1" × 4" material (each side equalling 24"). Make a groove in each side to hold the glass.
2. Cement aluminum foil to the 24" square of plywood so that it can act as a reflector.
3. Drill two ½" holes on one side piece for the copper tubing.
4. Nail five small cubes to the plywood to hold the sheet copper over the plywood.
5. Bend ⅜" copper tubing into a series of S-turns as shown in the diagram. At the same time, make the tubing lie as close as possible to the sheet copper.
6. Solder the copper tubing to the sheet copper. Then tack the sheet copper to the small cubes.
7. Attach the base to the sides with the glass in place. The collector box is now complete.
8. Drill a ¼" hole at points A1, B1, A, B, and at the screw cap on the top of the can.
9. Now solder two short lengths of ⅜" copper tubing to the five-gallon can at points A and B, which will be connected to points A1 and B1 by plastic tubing. Also, solder another ⅜" length to the screw cap on the top of the can.
10. Use ½" tubing for the cold water inlet. Attach a shut-off valve to the tube and extend another short length of ½" tubing from the valve. Solder the free end of the tubing to the inside of a brass hose fitting.
11. Set up the collector facing the sun and place the tank on a stand to keep it raised higher than the collector.
12. Fill the tank with the hose and notice how the circulating water is heated.

Note: Paint tubing, sheet copper, and can matte black. Substitute galvanized metal for copper to reduce the cost.

The solar water heater described above might be used by one household. (It obviously would not be appropriate on a very large scale.) The purpose of this example is to demonstrate the feasibility and the design requirements of a simple solar water heater. There are many designs available for more complex heaters.

'An enlarged version of the heater could be installed on a roof,

Worksheet

To employ means to use.

A *version* is a form or variation of an original. An *enlarged version* is a variation that is built on a large scale.

To install means to set up.

Permanent means lasting for ever; not temporary.

'An enlarged version of the heater could be installed on a roof, connected to a water supply, and used as a source of hot water.' Complete the following three sentences using the information from this sentence.

An enlarged version of the heater could be

....

An enlarged version of the heater could be

....

An enlarged version of the heater could be

....

" means inch or inches; *'* or *ft.* means foot or feet.

If something is *cut to size*, it is cut to fit the exact dimensions that are required.

A *valve* is a mechanical device that can be opened or closed to allow liquids or gases to flow or to stop them from flowing.

A *fitting* is an attachment.

Matte paint is the opposite of shiny paint. It does not reflect light.

A *hose* is a flexible pipe.

Direction vocabulary

A *groove* is a long narrow depression.

To reflect is to throw light back.

To bend is to curve or change the shape of something.

A *series* is a number of things of the same class coming one after another.

To solder is to melt a metal or metallic alloy to join two surfaces.

To assemble means to put pieces or parts together.

To be *in place* means to be in position.

To extend means to add something or make something longer.

A *tank* is a container.

To circulate means to flow or move around.

1. Prior to drilling two ½" holes on one side piece, we must:
   (a) Cement aluminum foil to the 24" square of plywood. ☐
   (b) Nail five small cubes to the plywood. ☐
   (c) Build the sides of the collector box. ☐
   (d) (a) and (c). ☐
   (e) None of the above. ☐

2. The ⅜" copper tubing is bent into a series of S-turns while simultaneously:
   (a) Five small cubes are nailed to the plywood. ☐
   (b) The tubing is made to lie as close as possible to the sheet copper. ☐
   (c) The copper tubing is soldered to the sheet. ☐
   (d) (a) and (c). ☐
   (e) None of the above. ☐

3. The copper tubing is soldered to the sheet. Subsequently:
   (a) The tubing is made to lie as close as possible to the sheet copper. ☐
   (b) The sheet copper is tacked to the small cubes. ☐
   (c) ⅜" copper tubing is bent into a series of S-turns. ☐
   (d) (a) and (c). ☐
   (e) None of the above. ☐

The latter is used to refer to the second or last object of a group that was previously mentioned. *The former* is used to refer to the first object of a group already mentioned. For example: 'Angelica and Maria are my students. The latter is from Spain. The former is from Argentina.' (Therefore, Maria is from Spain and Angelica is from Argentina.)

4. There are two main parts to a finished solar water heater, the five-gallon can and the collector box. The former must be raised above the latter in order for the hot water to rise. The former refers to:
   (a) The five-gallon can ☐
   (b) The collector box ☐
   (c) The solar water heater ☐
   (d) (a) and (b) ☐
   (e) None of the above ☐

Using the following words, fill in the blanks below:
is/are made of   consists of   contains   is/are filled with

5. The sides of the collector box .... wood.

6. The collector box .... tubing, sheet copper, aluminum foil, glass, and a wooden box.

7. The collector box .... copper tubing.

8. The five-gallon can .... water.

9. The five-gallon can .... metal.

10. The hosing connecting A to A1 .... plastic.

11. A solar water heater system .... a tank, a stand, hosing, and a collector box.

The following three sentences are different ways to tell about the function (use) of an object.
A solar water heater may be used to supply a permanent source of hot water.
A solar water heater may be used for supplying a permanent source of hot water.
A solar water heater may be used as a means of supplying a permanent source of hot water.

12. A collector box may be used for:
    (a) Extracting heat energy from the wind. ☐
    (b) Collecting waste products. ☐
    (c) Heating the water that passes through the copper tubing ☐
    (d) (a) and (c). ☐
    (e) None of the above. ☐

13. Write the sentence that you made in (12) in two other ways, using *may be used to* and *may be used as a means of*.

....

....

....

....

....

APPLY YOUR KNOWLEDGE *This exercise is for those students who have finished the worksheet before others in the class.*

Write a paragraph entitled *How to Construct a Solar Water Heater*. Use the directions on pages 94 and 96. Instead of numbering the directions, use vocabulary of chronological order.

....

....

....

....

....

....

....

....

....

....

....

....

....

Summary paragraphs

Look at the third paragraph in the reading. What is the purpose of this paragraph? It summarizes the first two paragraphs. When they write an article or a story, writers often summarize the main ideas of the whole article in the summarizing paragraph.

For students, a summarizing paragraph can be helpful in that:
Students can read the summary to get the main ideas of the paragraph if they do not have time to read the whole article.
Students can read the summary in order to review an article that they have already read but do not want to read again.
Students can read the summary to find out if the information they are looking for is in the article.

Students can read the summary to quickly separate the main ideas and the important ideas of the article from the details and unimportant information.

CHAPTER 9

Vocabulary

rapid	absence	bonus
to be in a rush	whereas	as a bonus
to compose	in this respect	sludge
to be composed of	to become excited	shortage
popular/popularity	manure	proposition
due to the fact that	to decompose	to generate
to threaten	tank	convenient
oil well	sealed	means
coal mine	airtight	disposal
swamp	to break down	to dispose
septic tank	trace	digestive system
to decay	to compress	a great deal

Grammar

I Compound sentence with *whereas*

II Reduced relative clauses

   A *which + be + verb form* becomes *Ø + Ø + verb form*

   B *which + simple present* becomes *Ø + Verb + ing*

III Sentences with *not . . . nor . . .*

IV Sentences with *not only . . . but also . . .*

Reading 9: Methane (bio-gas)

(1) We are in a rush to develop new sources of natural gas because our old sources are being rapidly used up. (2) Methane gas composes about 95 per cent of our natural gas. (3) Due to the fact that natural gas burns cleanly and efficiently, it is one of our most popular fuels. (4) It is this popularity that threatens our supplies of this gas.

(5) Methane gas is a fossil fuel, found in oil wells and coal mines. (6) However, it is also found in swamps, septic tanks, and the digestive systems of animals. (7) It is produced by the decay of organic matter in the absence of oxygen whereas coal and oil are only produced when under extreme heat and pressure. (8) In this respect, methane is different from coal and oil. (9) Once coal and oil are used up, they are not easy to manufacture again, but it is easy to manufacture new supplies of methane.

(10) Many people are becoming excited by the idea of producing their own methane. (11) This is done by allowing manure and other organic wastes to decompose in a sealed tank called a digester. (12) Bacteria break down the organic matter. (13) This produces a mixture of methane, carbon dioxide, and traces of other gases. (14) This mixture, containing from 50 percent to 70 percent methane, is called bio-gas.

(15) Bio-gas can be used for the same purposes as natural gas, that is, cooking, heating, and lighting. (16) It can also be compressed for use in internal combustion engines. (17) Unfortunately, it takes a great deal of work to compress the gas, so that is not an efficient use of this energy. (18) As a bonus to providing energy, the sludge left in the digester when it has stopped producing gas makes a good fertilizer.

(19) The methane digester is not a total solution to the energy shortage, nor is it a practical proposition for a single, small family. (20) The organic wastes from a single, small family are too limited in quantity to generate much energy. (21) A farm or a place where large groups of people live are perfect places for methane digesters. (22) The digester supplies not only fuel and fertilizer, but also a convenient means for disposal of manure.

Worksheet

Sentence 1

Rapid means quick.

1. A paraphrase of sentence (1) is (use context clues to think of a meaning for 'to be in a rush'):
   (a) We have a lot of time to develop new sources of natural gas because our old sources are being rapidly used up. ☐
   (b) We are inside a rush where new sources of natural gas are developed because our old sources are being rapidly used up. ☐
   (c) We must develop new sources of natural gas quickly because our old sources are being rapidly used up. ☐
   (d) None of the above. ☐

2. There are two clauses in sentence (1). One clause tells the reason; the other clause tells the result. Which is the reason clause?

   .... Which is the result

   clause? ....

Sentence 2

To compose means to be a part of; to make up.

1. A paraphrase of sentence (2) is:
   (a) About 95 per cent of our natural gas is composed of methane. ☐
   (b) About 95 per cent of our natural gas composes methane. ☐
   (c) About 95 per cent is composed methane of our natural gas. ☐
   (d) (a) and (b). ☐
   (e) None of the above. ☐

2. *To compose* is an active verb. *To be composed of* is a passive verb. When we use *be composed of*, the whole substance comes first, and then the parts come second. When we use the active form, the parts of the whole come first. Replace the blanks with *is/are composed of* or *compose(s)*.

Fossil fuels .... vegetation, timber, and other organic materials. Vegetation, timber, and other organic materials

.... fossil fuels.

Sentence 3

Popular means well-liked.

1. *Due to the fact that* can be replaced by *because*. Rewrite the sentence with *because*.

....

....

2. Which is the reason clause?

....

Which is the result clause?

....

Sentence 4

To threaten means to endanger; to put in danger.

1. 'Popularity' is the .... form of *popular*.
   - (a) Adjective (describing someone or something that is well-liked) ☐
   - (b) Verb (to be well-liked) ☐
   - (c) Noun (the state of being popular, well-liked) ☐

PARAGRAPH 1
Which of the following questions most generally summarizes the ideas in paragraph (1)?
   - (a) Why are we in a rush? ☐
   - (b) Why is there a need for methane gas? ☐
   - (c) What are some new sources of natural gas? ☐
   - (d) What percentage of our natural gas is methane gas? ☐

Sentence 5

An *oil well* is a structure for drawing oil out of the ground.
A *coal mine* is a hole in the earth from which coal is extracted.

Sentence 6

A *swamp* is wet land which is covered with water in areas.

A *septic tank* is a container in which solid waste products are decomposed by bacteria.

Digestive system comes from the verb *to digest*. *To digest* means to convert the food we eat into energy and waste products. A *digestive system* consists of the parts of a body that do this job.

Sentence 7

1. 'It' refers to:
   (a) Fossil fuels ☐
   (b) Animals ☐
   (c) Methane ☐
2. 'Decay of organic matter' means:
   (a) Decomposition of organic matter ☐
   (b) Composition of organic matter ☐
   (c) Growth of organic matter ☐

Absent means not present; not available. *Absence* is the noun form of *absent*.

3. Organic matter includes (check as many as are correct):
   (a) Flowers ☐
   (b) Animals ☐
   (c) People ☐
   (d) Vegetables ☐
   (e) Stone ☐

Whereas means on the other hand, on the contrary. It contrasts two sentences.

Sentence 8

1. *In this respect* means in this way. 'This respect' refers to:
   (a) Methane is found in oil wells and coal mines. ☐
   (b) Methane gas is a fossil fuel. ☐
   (c) Methane can be produced in the absence of oxygen without pressure or heat. ☐
   (d) (b) and (c). ☐

Sentence 9

1. Which word could replace 'but' in the sentence?
   (a) Therefore ☐
   (b) However ☐
   (c) Because ☐

PARAGRAPH 2

Which of the following questions most generally summarizes the ideas in paragraph (2)?

(a) Why is there a need for methane? ☐

(b) What are some similarities and differences between methane and other fossil fuels? ☐

(c) Where is methane found? ☐

(d) Why is our supply of methane threatened? ☐

Sentence 10

To become excited by something means to be very interested in it.

Sentence 11

Manure is the solid waste product of animals.
Decompose means to return back to an original state. (The prefix *de-* means the opposite process.)

1. *Oxidize* means to combine with oxygen. What do you think *de-*

   oxidize means? ....

A *tank* is a kind of container.
Sealed means *airtight* (air cannot enter).

2. 'This' refers to:
   (a) Becoming excited ☐
   (b) Producing methane on our own ☐
   (c) Many people ☐

3. Why do we need a sealed tank? (Look for the answer in sentence 7.)

   ....

4. A digester is a place where ....

Sentences 12 and 13

To break down means to divide into original parts; to decompose.
A *trace* is a very small amount.

1. Using the information from sentences (12) and (13), complete the following sentences:

Prior to producing a mixture of methane, CO_2 and traces of other gases,

....

After the bacteria break down the organic matter,

....

....

2. What chemicals does bio-gas contain?

....

PARAGRAPH 3

Which of the following questions most generally summarizes paragraph (3)?

  (a) Why are people excited about producing their own methane? □

  (b) How is bio-gas produced? □

  (c) Do people want to produce their own methane? □

  (d) What is the make-up of methane? □

Sentence 15

1. Bio-gas can be used as a means of ...., ..., and ....

Sentence 16

To compress means to apply pressure to something.

Sentence 17

A *great deal* means a lot; in a large amount.

1. 'That' refers to:

  (a) Use in cooking □

  (b) Use in internal combustion engines □

  (c) Use in heating □

  (d) None of the above □

Sentence 18

A *bonus* is something extra. *As a bonus* means in addition.

Sludge is a muddy (mud-like) substance.

PARAGRAPH 4
Which of the following questions most generally summarizes
  paragraph 4?
  (a) How can we produce bio-gas and natural gas? ☐
  (b) How can we use natural gas? ☐
  (c) What are some practical and impractical uses that result
      from the production of bio-gas? ☐

Sentence 19

A *shortage* of something means too small a supply of something.
A *proposition* is an idea.

1. A paraphrase of sentence (19) is (a sentence with *not . . . nor . . .* contains at least two negative sentences):
   (a) The methane digester is not a total solution to the energy
       shortage but it is a practical proposition for a single,
       small family. ☐
   (b) The methane digester is not a total solution to the energy
       shortage; therefore, it is not a practical idea for a single,
       small family. ☐
   (c) The methane digester is not a total solution to the energy
       shortage and it is also not a practical idea for a single,
       small family. ☐

Sentence 20

To generate is to produce.

1. Why isn't a methane digester practical for a single, small family?

....

....

....

....

....

....

   (Make sure your sentence is complete, i.e. a sentence with *because*
   must have a reason *and* a result clause.)

Sentence 22

Convenient means easy to use.
A *means* is a way; a method.
Disposal is the noun form of *to dispose*. *To dispose* means to throw away; to get rid of.

1. A paraphrase of sentence (22) is (a sentence with *not only . . . but also . . .* has two clauses. The first clause contains information. The second clause contains added information):
   (a) The digester supplies fuel and fertilizer but isn't a convenient way to dispose of manure. ☐
   (b) The digester supplies only fertilizer and not fuel but it is a convenient way to dispose of manure. ☐
   (c) The digester supplies fuel and fertilizer and in addition, it is a convenient means for disposal of manure. ☐

PARAGRAPH 5
Paragraph (5) states some conclusions about the use of digesters. Which of the following are not conclusions? (Choose one or more than one answer.)
   (a) A small, family home is a perfect place for a digester. ☐
   (b) Methane gas can be used for all our energy needs. ☐
   (c) Using a digester is a good method of getting rid of manure. ☐
   (d) Energy and fertilizer are two useful products of a methane digester. ☐

Outline

On your worksheet, you chose a question that best summarized each paragraph. *Write this question next to the* I, II, III *and* IV *below. Fill in the rest of the blanks.*

I ....

   A ....

      1. Methane gas composes 95 per cent of our natural gas.
      2. It is our most popular fuel.

         (a) ....

         (b) Because it burns efficiently

II ....

   A Similarities

      1. ....

   B ....

      1. ....

      2. Also produced by the decay of organic matter in the absence of oxygen whereas coal and oil are produced only under pressure.

      3. ....

III ....

   A Bacteria break down organic matter in a sealed tank.

   B ....

   C This mixture of gases is called bio-gas.

IV ....

A Practical uses
  1. Cooking

  2. ....

  3. ....

  4. The sludge can be used as fertilizer.

B ....
  1. Use in internal combustion engines

    (a) Because ....

V Some conclusions we can make about the use of digesters:
  A Methane gas is not a total solution to the energy shortage.

  B ....
    1. Because the wastes from a small family are too limited in quantity to generate much energy

  C We can use digesters on farms or places where large groups of people live.

  D A methane digester supplies many things.
    1. Energy

    2. ....

    3. A convenient means for disposing of manure

Grammar—reduced relative clauses

The following grammar lesson is a continuation of the lesson on relative clauses on pages 59 to 61. Go back to that lesson if you feel that you need review.

Look at sentence (11) in the reading: 'This is done by allowing manure and other organic wastes to decompose in a sealed tank called a digester.' What does 'called a digester' refer to? Why is the verb in the past participle form? To answer these questions, we must realize that the sentence above is reduced from: 'This is done by allowing manure and other organic wastes to decompose in a sealed tank *which is* called a digester.'

It is, in reality, a sentence with a relative clause. Now, what does

'which is called a digester' refer to? ....

Why was the verb in the past participle form? ....

.... Which words were dropped in the

reduced sentence? ....

Look at sentence (5): 'Methane gas is a fossil fuel, found in oil wells and coal mines.' Why is 'found' in the past participle form?

.... We can rewrite the sentence as follows: 'Methane gas is a fossil fuel, which is found in oil wells and coal mines.'

Look at sentence (18): 'As a bonus to providing energy, the sludge left in the digester when it has stopped producing gas makes a good

fertilizer.' Why is 'left' in the past participle form? ....

.... Rewrite the sentence adding *which is* in the proper position.

....

....

The rule for reducing relative clauses is: if you have a sentence with a relative clause which has the form *which + be + verb form*, you can drop *which + be*.

Which verbs have the form *be + verb form*?
1. Passive verbs (as in sentences (5), (11) and (18))
2. Progressive tense verbs (*is going, was going*, etc.)
   Here is an example of a sentence with a relative clause in the progressive form:
'A windmill which is rotating in a wind at 8.1 meters/second can produce two horsepowers of energy.'
Because there is *which + be (is) + verb form (rotating)*, we can drop the *which + be (is)* and reduce the sentence:
'A windmill rotating in a wind at 8.1 meters/second can produce two horsepowers of energy.'

Is this a sentence with a defining or a non-defining clause?

.... Do all windmills rotate in a wind at 8.1 meters/second or does this sentence *only* refer to a certain windmill, one that rotates in a wind at 8.1 meters/second?

....

Exercises
Choose the correct sentence with a reduced relative clause that is a paraphrase of the two given sentences. For example:
Water must be abundant and available throughout the year.
This water is used to produce electricity.
(a) Water, used to produce electricity, must be abundant and available throughout the year. ☐
(b) Water used to produce electricity must be abundant and available throughout the year. ☐
(c) Water is used to produce electricity must be abundant and available throughout the year. ☐
(d) None of the above. ☐

   First, we rewrite the sentence as a sentence with a complete relative clause. 'Water which is used to produce electricity must be abundant and available throughout the year.' 'Which is used' has the same form as *which + be + verb form* so we can reduce the sentence. (c) is wrong because the *be* was not dropped. (a) and (b) are the same except that the former is non-defining and the latter is defining. We are only talking about water that produces electricity and not all water. Therefore, the sentence should have a defining clause; (b) is correct.

115

1. Organic wastes produce bio-gas.
   These organic wastes are broken down by bacteria in the absence of oxygen.
   (a) Organic wastes broken down by bacteria in the absence of oxygen produce bio-gas. ☐
   (b) Organic wastes which broken down by bacteria in the absence of oxygen produce bio-gas. ☐
   (c) Organic wastes are broken down by bacteria in the absence of oxygen produce bio-gas. ☐
   (d) None of the above. ☐

2. We need a knowledge of grammar in order to understand a language.
   Grammar is difficult.
   (a) We need a knowledge of grammar, difficult, in order to understand a language. ☐
   (b) We need a knowledge of grammar, is difficult, in order to understand a language. ☐
   (c) We need a knowledge of grammar, which difficult, in order to understand a language. ☐
   (d) None of the above. ☐
   (*Hint:* Is 'difficult' a verb?)

3. Careless disposal of waste products increases pollution.
   Pollution is making our water undrinkable and our air unbreathable.
   (a) Careless disposal of waste products increases pollution, is making our water undrinkable and our air unbreathable. ☐
   (b) Careless disposal of waste products increases pollution, making our water undrinkable and our air-unbreathable. ☐
   (c) Careless disposal of waste products increases pollution making our water undrinkable and our air unbreathable. ☐
   (d) None of the above. ☐

4. A methane digester is a sealed tank.
   A methane digester is used to break down organic matter.
   (a) A methane digester, used to break down organic matter, is a sealed tank. ☐
   (b) A methane digester is used to break down organic matter, is a sealed tank. ☐

(c) A methane digester used to break down organic matter is a sealed tank. ☐

(d) None of the above. ☐

Exercises (5)–(8) *Break down the given sentences into two or more sentences.*

5. A methane digester supplied with organic wastes from a farm will provide adequate quantities of both fuel and fertilizer.
   (a) A methane digester will provide adequate quantities of both fuel and fertilizer. This methane digester is supplied with organic wastes from a farm. ☐
   (b) A methane digester is supplied with organic wastes from a farm. A farm will provide adequate quantities of both fuel and fertilizer. ☐
   (c) A methane digester will provide adequate quantities of both fuel and fertilizers. A methane digester supplied organic wastes to a farm. ☐
   (d) A methane digester will provide adequate quantities of organic wastes for a farm. A methane digester is supplied with both fuel and fertilizers. ☐

6. A book written for engineering students should contain both technical and general vocabulary.
   (a) A book is written for engineering students. A book should contain both technical and general vocabulary. ☐
   (b) If a book is written for engineering students, it should contain both technical and general vocabulary. ☐
   (c) A book is written for engineering students. Engineering students should contain both technical and general vocabulary. ☐
   (d) None of the above. ☐

7. UNICEF, helping children all over the world, is a project of the United Nations.
   (a) UNICEF is a project of the United Nations. UNICEF is helping children all over the world. ☐
   (b) Children help UNICEF all over the world. UNICEF is a project of the United Nations. ☐
   (c) UNICEF is helping children all over the world. The world is a project of the United Nations. ☐
   (d) None of the above. ☐

8. Bio-gas, composed of methane, CO_2, and traces of other gases, can be generated easily and quickly.
   - (a) Bio-gas is composed of methane, CO_2, and traces of other gases. Other gases can be generated easily and quickly. ☐
   - (b) Bio-gas, methane, CO_2, and traces of other gases can all be generated easily and quickly. ☐
   - (c) Bio-gas can be generated easily and quickly. Easily and quickly are composed of methane, CO_2, and traces of other gases. ☐
   - (d) None of the above. ☐

Look at sentence (14) in the reading: 'This mixture, containing from 50 percent to 70 percent methane, is called bio-gas.' This sentence is a reduced form of the following: 'This mixture, which contains from 50 percent to 70 percent methane, is called bio-gas.'

Therefore, in a sentence with a relative clause of the form *which + simple present*, we can drop the *which* and change the verb to the *-ing* form.

To summarize reduced relative clauses, often when you see a verb in the *-ing* form or the past participle form without any auxiliary, it is part of a reduced relative clause. There are two ways to reduce a relative clause:
1. If the relative clause is in the form *which + be + verb form* (i.e. passive or progressive tense), we can drop the *which + be*.
2. If the relative clause is in the form *which + simple present*, we can drop the *which* and change the verb to its *-ing* form.

Check the correct paraphrase.

9. A methane digester producing natural gas for a farm needs to be maintained and regularly supplied with new organic wastes.
   - (a) A methane digester producing natural gas for a farm. This farm needs to be maintained and regularly supplied with new organic wastes. ☐
   - (b) A methane digester produces natural gas for a farm. This farm needs to be maintained and regularly supplied with new organic wastes. ☐
   - (c) A methane digester needs to be maintained and regularly supplied with new organic wastes. This methane digester produces natural gas for a farm. ☐
   - (d) None of the above. ☐

10. A solar water heater supplying hot water to a small family must have a capacity of at least 100 liters.
    (a) A solar water heater must have a capacity of at least 100 liters. That solar water heater supplies hot water to a small family. ☐
    (b) If a solar water heater supplies hot water to a small family, it must have a capacity of at least 100 liters. ☐
    (c) All solar water heaters must have a capacity of at least 100 liters. All solar water heaters supply water to small families. ☐
    (d) (a) and (b). ☐
    (e) None of the above. ☐

11. To build a methane digester, a pit must be dug.
    This pit measures ten to twelve feet deep.
    (a) To build a methane digester, a pit measures ten to twelve feet deep must be dug. ☐
    (b) To build a methane digester, a pit is measuring ten to twelve feet deep must be dug. ☐
    (c) To build a methane digester, a pit measuring ten to twelve feet deep must be dug. ☐

12. Pakistan may find appropriate technology useful.
    Pakistan has a mostly rural population.
    (a) Pakistan, having a mostly rural population, may find appropriate technology useful. ☐
    (b) Pakistan, having a mostly rural population, may find appropriate technology useful. ☐
    (c) Pakistan having a mostly rural population may find appropriate technology useful. ☐
    (d) None of the above. ☐

For more practice, turn to pages 61 to 63 and try to reduce the sentences with relative clauses there.

Vocabulary

Fill in the blanks or replace the words in italics with words from the vocabulary.

1. A methane digester should be .... to prevent oxygen from getting in.

2. Manure is .... by the bacteria into a mixture of methane, CO_2 and traces of other gases.

3. Bio-gas .... methane, CO_2 and traces of other gases.

4. If there is an .... of oxygen, bio-gas can be formed. However, if oxygen is present, bio-gas cannot be formed.

5. If there is a wood .... this winter, many people will be cold.

6. Pollution is caused by poor .... of waste products.

7. A methane digester produces bio-gas. *In addition*, the sludge can

   be used as fertilizer. ....

8. A methane digester is not good for a single, small family *because* they only produce a limited quantity of waste products.

   ....

9. Fossil fuels sometimes produce pollution; *on the contrary*, a methane digester uses waste products which could cause

   pollution. ....

10. We can't allow even a *small amount* of oxygen to enter the tank where the waste products are being broken down.

....

Constructing a bio-gas digester in China

CHAPTER 10

Vocabulary

to chop	hosing	by means of
to destroy	poles	to fasten
destruction	joints	to conduct
barrel	to drain	

Grammar

Relative clauses with prepositions

Skills

Following diagrams along with instructions

Reading 10: Installation and maintenance of a methane digester (Part 1)

As you read this reading, refer to the diagram. After some of the directions, you will see written 'diagram ....'. *Write in the number of the diagram that refers to that sentence.*

(1) Part of the solution to the energy crisis might be the methane digester. (2) Decreasing supplies of firewood are a problem in many parts of the world today. (3) Chopping down trees for fuel leads to destruction of natural resources. (4) By building a methane generator which uses human and animal waste products, people can produce fuel as well as fertilizer and reduce their dependence on firewood as their main source of fuel.

(5) The materials needed for the installation of a gas generator are as follows: seven large metal barrels (diagram ....), rubber hosing, five wooden poles, large stones (or bricks), chicken wire (if available), mud (or concrete mixed with mud), strong wire, nine small pieces of threaded pipe (diagram ....), one metal tap (diagram

............), three four-holed joints to which threaded pipes may be

joined (diagram ....), and one long metal pipe.

(6) Cut the bottoms off the seven barrels. (7) Most barrels containing liquid have holes on top, to which taps may be attached, in order to drain out the liquid. (Find these holes in diagram 2.)

(8) To these holes, you should attach the small pieces of threaded pipe. (9) If you cannot attach the pipes by means of screw threads, you will have to weld the parts together. (10) After this, fasten all seven barrels together by means of strong wire or welding (diagram ....). (11) Attach one four-holed joint to the center barrel (diagram ....). (12) Attach two four-holed joints to the center four-holed joint (diagram ....). (13) Rubber hosing should be connected to the barrels and the four-holed joints (diagram ....). (14) Attach the tap to the top of the center four-holed joint (diagram ....). (15) To the tap, fix the rubber hose that will conduct the gas to your cooking stove. (Put an x next to the hose in diagram 3 that will be connected to the cooking stove.)

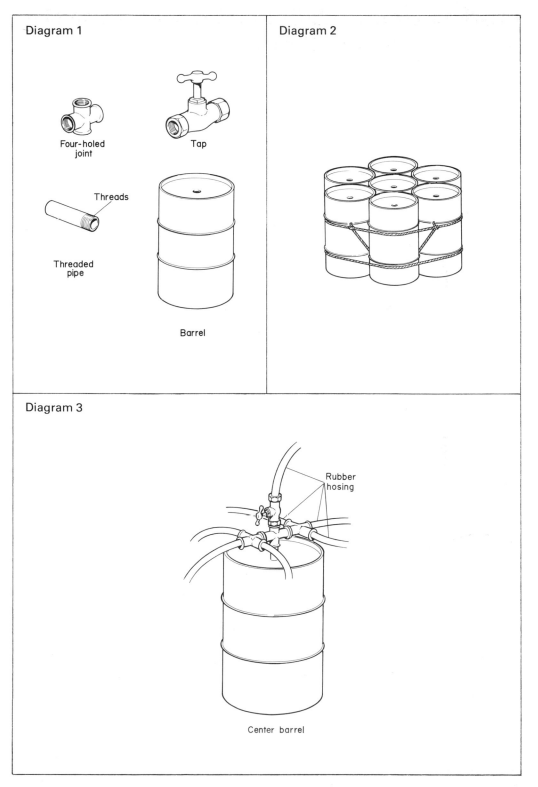

Diagram 1

Four-holed joint

Tap

Threads

Threaded pipe

Barrel

Diagram 2

Diagram 3

Rubber hosing

Center barrel

Worksheet

Sentence 3

To chop means to cut.
To destroy means to ruin. (A fire destroys wooden houses easily.)

1. 'Destruction' is the .... form of *to destroy*.
   (a) Adjective (describing something that is ruined) ☐
   (b) Noun (the state of being in ruin) ☐
   (c) Verb (to ruin) ☐

2. A fire can cause .... to wooden houses easily. Which would

   you use here, *destruction* or *destroy*? ....

PARAGRAPH 1

1. Which sentence numbers describe the disadvantages of using

   firewood? .... and ....

2. Which of the following might be reasons to use methane instead
   of firewood?
   (a) Supplies of firewood are decreasing. ☐
   (b) Using firewood destroys natural resources. ☐
   (c) With a methane generator, people can get fuel and fer-
       tilizer at the same time. ☐
   (d) All of the above. ☐

3. Another way to say 'By building a methane gas generator which
   uses human and animal waste products, people can product fuel
   as well as fertilizer' is:
   (a) By building a methane gas generator using human and
       animal waste products, people can produce neither fuel
       nor fertilizer. ☐
   (b) By building a methane gas generator using human and
       animal waste products, people can produce fuel and
       fertilizer. ☐
   (c) By building a methane gas generator using human and
       animal waste products, people can produce fuel but not
       fertilizer. ☐

Sentence 5

1. Why is 'needed' in the past participle form? ....

.... Write out the sentence using a complete relative clause.

....

A *barrel* is a cylindrical container.
Hosing is flexible piping.
Poles are sticks or rods.
Joints are the places where two things or parts are joined; the pieces that join two things or parts.

Sentence 7

1. A paraphrase of sentence (7) is:
   (a) Most barrels contain liquid. Most barrels have holes on top. Taps may be attached to these holes in order to drain out liquid.   ☐
   (b) All barrels have holes on top. These barrels contain liquid. To the holes on top, we may attach taps to drain out the liquid.   ☐
   (c) Most barrels which contain liquid have holes on top. Taps may be attached to these holes in order to drain out liquid.   ☐
   (d) (b) and (c).   ☐
   (e) None of the above.   ☐

To drain means to draw liquid out.

Sentence 9

By means of is by way of.

Sentence 10

1. Look at diagram 2. The barrels are *fastened* together. What do you think *to fasten* means? ....

Sentence 15

To conduct means to lead or act as a passage for something.

127

Grammar—relative clauses with objects and prepositions

In Chapter 5, you learned about relative clauses.

I see the book. + The book is red. = I see the book which is red.

The common words are 'the book'. We place the second sentence following the repeating words. Finally, we replace the repeating words with a relative pronoun *which*. Look at these two sentences:

I see the book. + I need the book.

The common words are again 'the book'. Look what happens, however, if we place the second sentence following the repeating words and use *which*: 'I see the book I need which'. This is obviously wrong. If you remember Chapter 5, you learned that the relative pronoun always comes at the beginning of the relative clause:

I see the book *which I need*.

Choose the correct paraphrases of the following:

1. Bio-gas is composed of methane, carbon dioxide, and traces of other gases.
   Digesters can produce bio-gas.
   (a) Bio-gas, which digesters can produce, is composed of methane, carbon dioxide, and traces of other gases. ☐
   (b) Bio-gas which can produce digesters is composed of methane, carbon dioxide, and traces of other gases. ☐
   (c) Bio-gas digesters can produce which, is composed of methane, carbon dioxide, and traces of other gases. ☐
   (d) None of the above. ☐

2. Mechanical drawing involves preparing and reading diagrams.
   Architects need to study mechanical drawing.
   (a) Mechanical drawing, architects need to study which, involves preparing and reading designs. ☐
   (b) Mechanical drawing, which architects need to study, involves preparing and reading designs. ☐
   (c) Mechanical drawing which involves preparing and reading designs needs architects to study. ☐
   (d) None of the above. ☐

3. The technology of solar energy, which scientists have not yet perfected, is a new field of science.
   (a) The technology of solar energy is a new field of science. The technology of solar energy has not yet perfected scientists. ☐
   (b) The technology of solar energy is a new field of science. Scientists have not yet perfected the technology of solar energy. ☐
   (c) Science is a new field of solar energy. Scientists are not yet perfected. ☐
   (d) None of the above. ☐

4. Air pollution, which careless industries cause, is abundant in New York.
   (a) Air pollution causes careless industries. Careless industries are abundant in New York. ☐
   (b) Careless industries cause air pollution. Air pollution causes New York. ☐
   (c) Air pollution is abundant in New York. Careless industries cause air pollution. ☐
   (d) None of the above. ☐

Sometimes the verbs in the relative clauses have prepositions. For example:

I need the book. + I am studying from the book.

We can say, as one possibility, 'I need the book which I am studying from.' (Notice that here, again, we have to bring *which* to the front of the relative clause because it replaces the object of the second sentence.) A second possibility is: 'I need the book from which I am studying.' (Notice that here, instead of moving *which* to the front of the relative clause, we moved both the preposition *from* and *which*.)
   Therefore, when making relative clauses with verbs + prepositions, you can do two things. You can leave the preposition with the verb or you can bring the preposition to the front of the relative clause along with the relative pronoun.

5. The center barrel should be fastened securely to the other barrels. A four-holed joint should be attached to the centre barrel.
   (a) The center barrel, which a four-holed joint should be attached to, should be fastened securely to the other barrels. ☐

(b) The center barrel, to which a four-holed joint should be attached, should be fastened securely to the other barrels. ☐

(c) The center barrel, a four-holed joint should be attached to which, should be fastened securely to the other barrels. ☐☐

(d) (a) and (b). ☐

6. Fossil fuels may soon be exhausted.
   Developing countries depend on fossil fuels.

   (a) Fossil fuels, which developing countries depend on, may soon be exhausted. ☐

   (b) Fossil fuels, developing countries depend on which, may soon be exhausted. ☐

   (c) Fossil fuels, on which developing countries depend, may soon be exhausted. ☐☐

   (d) (a) and (c).

   (c) A stand can be made of wood or metal. A stand the tank of a solar water heater is supported by. ☐☐

   (d) None of the above.

7. A stand by which the tank of a solar water heater is supported can be made of wood or metal.

   (a) A stand can be made of wood or metal. The tank of a solar water heater is supported by a stand. ☐

   (b) A stand can be made of wood or metal. A stand is supported by the tank of a solar water heater. ☐

8. The water with which the tank is filled heats by circulating through the copper tubing.

   (a) The water heats by circulating through the copper tubing. The water is filled with the tank. ☐

   (b) The water heats by circulating through the copper tubing. The tank is filled with this water. ☐

   (c) The water with the tank is filled. The tank is heated by circulating water through the copper tubing. ☐☐

   (d) None of the above.

Let us return to sentence (7) in the reading: 'Most barrels containing liquid have holes on top, to which taps may be attached, in order to drain out the liquid.' There are two relative clauses in this sentence: 'Most barrels *which contain liquid* have holes on top, *to which taps may be attached*, in order to drain out the liquid.'

The first part of the sentence may be paraphrased as follows: 'Most barrels have holes on top in order to drain out the liquid. These barrels contain liquid.'

The second part of the sentence may be paraphrased as follows: 'Most barrels have holes on top in order to drain out the liquid. Taps may be attached to these holes on top.' In this second part, the preposition was moved to the front of the relative clause along with *which*. We can also say the sentence as follows (leaving the preposition with the verb and moving only *which*): 'Most barrels which contain liquid have holes on top, *which taps may be attached to*, in order to drain out the liquid.'

Bio-gas digesters in Nepal

CHAPTER 11

Vocabulary

pit	fittings	build-up
to dig	to function	scum
to line	properly	to drive
to sink	to escape	forked
to prevent	to agitate	to expel
channelway	to enhance	to overflow

Vocabulary of spatial order

Grammar

I Paragraph organization

  A Paragraph organized according to spatial order

  B Paragraph organized according to spatial and chronological order at the same time

Reading 11: Installation and maintenance of a methane digester (Part 2)

(16) A pit of equal diameter to the joined barrels plus 6" should be dug (diagram ....). (17) The depth of the pit should be ten to twelve feet. (18) (Smaller digesters, which produce less gas, may be more useful for small families.) (19) The wall of the pit must be lined with bricks or stones (and chicken wire, if available) and mud or mud mixed with concrete (diagram ....). (20) Measure down the pit a distance equal to the height of the barrels and put a horizontal iron bar or pipe at that depth to prevent the barrels from sinking down to the bottom. (Mark this horizontal bar with an x in diagram 4.) (21) Line the top of the pit with stone and mud also, and make a small channelway to another hole, lined one foot deep by two feet wide by two feet long (diagram ....). (22) Fill the large pit with a mixture of cow manure and water to the ratio of 1:1. (23) Place the barrels with all the necessary fittings into the pit. (24) To make the gas digester function properly, make sure all the fittings are airtight to avoid the escape of gas.

(25) We also need to build a construction to agitate the manure and water mixture by turning the barrels. (26) Agitation of the mixture enhances the production of methane and prevents the build-up of scum which could slow down or stop gas generation. (27) To build this construction, first drive one forked wooden pole into the ground on one side of the large pit and drive another forked pole into the ground on the other side (diagram ....). (28) One large pole is placed so that it rests on the forks of the vertical wooden poles. (Mark the pole that rests on the vertical poles with an x in diagram 6.) (29) Lastly, two long poles are attached to the long horizontal pole so that the poles extend into the spaces between the barrels in the pit. (Mark each pole with an o.) (30) These poles are used to turn the barrels and thus agitate the manure and water mixture.

(31) The barrels in the pit should be full of gas in about two weeks' time. (32) This is noticeable by the rising of the tanks within the pit. (33) Once a mixture has produced gas, it is no longer usable for more gas production. (34) Therefore, in order to continue methane generation, new manure and water must be added to the old mixture every few days. (35) The mixture which has expelled its gas will overflow into the smaller pit. (36) This used mixture is rich in nitrogen and is excellent for use as fertilizer. (37) Consequently, continuous feeding of the digester leads to a continuous supply of both energy and fertilizer.

Vocabulary

Sentence 16

A *pit* is a large hole in the ground.
To dig means to remove dirt from the ground to form a hole.

Sentence 19

To line something means to cover its inner surface.

Sentence 20

To sink means to fall or drop to a lower level.
To prevent means to avoid; to stop something from happening.

Sentence 21

A *channelway* is a small passage leading from one place to another.

Sentence 23

Fittings are attachments.

Sentence 24

To function means to work; to be put to use.
Properly means correctly; in the correct way.
To escape means to get out (usually secretively).

Sentence 25

To agitate means to shake something or move something around.

Sentence 26

To enhance something means to make it better.
A *build-up* is a growth or concentration of a material.
Scum is the waste matter which solidifies and forms on the surface of a liquid.

Sentence 27

To drive something into the ground means to push it into the ground using a lot of strength.
Something that is *forked* branches from one part into two parts.

Sentence 35

To expel means to send out.
To overflow means to flow over; to go over the capacity of a container.

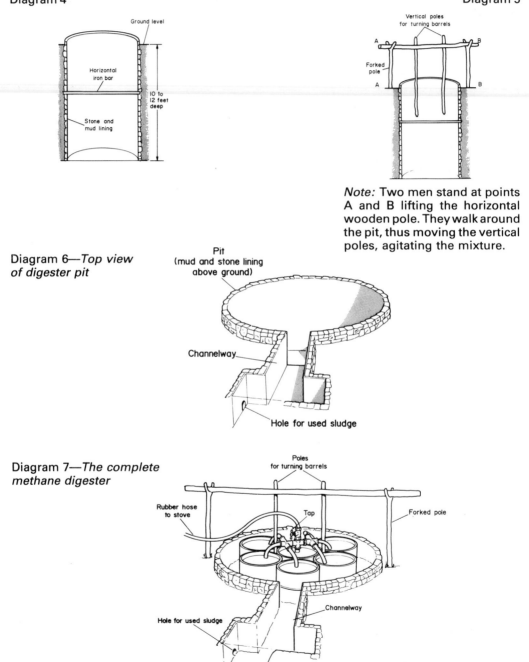

Diagram 4

Diagram 5

Note: Two men stand at points A and B lifting the horizontal wooden pole. They walk around the pit, thus moving the vertical poles, agitating the mixture.

Diagram 6—*Top view of digester pit*

Diagram 7—*The complete methane digester*

Reading comprehension

Answer each of the following by checking the most complete and correct answer. Refer to parts 1 and 2 of *Installation and Maintenance of a Methane Digester.*

1. In this project, a .... is installed.
   (a) Solar collector box
   (b) Methane gas generator
   (c) Means of producing fertilizer
   (d) (b) and (c)
   (e) None of the above

2. The seven metal barrels are used for ....
   (a) Holding the manure and water mixture
   (b) Collecting and storing methane gas
   (c) Mixing mud with concrete
   (d) None of the above

3. The large pit is used for ....
   (a) Holding the manure and water mixture
   (b) Collecting sunlight
   (c) Generating methane gas
   (d) (a) and (c)
   (e) None of the above

4. The tap is used for ....
   (a) Controlling the movement of the manure and water mixture
   (b) Controlling the flow of gas from the barrels to the cooking stove
   (c) Controlling the amount of sunlight in the pit
   (d) None of the above

5. The fittings (the hoses and pipes) must be tight so that

   ....
   (a) Manure and water can't get out
   (b) Sunlight can't get out
   (c) Bacteria can't get out
   (d) None of the above

6. The .... produce(s) the methane gas.
   (a) Mud in the walls of the pit
   (b) Manure and water mixture
   (c) Bacteria
   (d) (b) and (c)
   (e) None of the above

7. The wooden poles are used for ....
   (a) Making music
   (b) Agitating the manure and water mixture
   (c) Keeping sunlight out of the pit
   (d) (b) and (c)
   (e) None of the above

8. Agitation (movement) of the manure and water mixture is neces-

   sary to ....
   (a) Improve the production of methane
   (b) Prevent the production of methane
   (c) Stop the growth of scum on the surface of the mixture
   (d) (a) and (c)
   (e) None of the above

9. New mixtures of manure and water must be added to the mixture

   because ....
   (a) The old mixture can only produce gas once
   (b) New mixtures are necessary to continue gas produc-
       tion
   (c) The old mixture evaporates
   (d) (a) and (b)
   (e) None of the above

10. The mixture which has already given off (expelled) its gas can be

    used ....
    (a) To produce more gas
    (b) As fertilizer
    (c) (a) and (b)
    (d) None of the above

Grammar—spatial order

The following paragraph is a brief description of the building of a methane digester. *According to the information from the two preceding readings, fill in the blanks with the following words*. They may be used more than once.

together	into which	to the right	on the surface of
deep	adjacent to (next to)	between	bottom of
over	vertically	in	on top of
horizontal	interior	below	to the left
to the top of			

First, remove the bottoms from the barrels. Second, fasten the barrels (1) .... Next, attach the necessary fittings (2) .... the barrels. After that, a pit should be dug (3) .... the ground. The pit should be dug ten to twelve feet (4) .... The (5) .... of the pit should be lined with stones and mud. A (6) .... iron bar should be placed in the pit. This bar is placed directly (7) .... the barrels to keep them from sinking to the (8) .... the pit. (9) .... the large pit a small hole is dug (10) .... the used sludge is emptied. Subsequently, the large pit is filled with a mixture of cow manure and water, and the barrels are placed (11) .... the mixture. Finally, we must build a structure which will be used to agitate the mixture. One forked pole is driven into the ground (12) .... of the pit and another forked pole is placed (13) .... of the pit. One (14) .... pole is placed on the forked poles so that it rests (15) .... the pit. Two poles are attached to the horizontal pole so that they extend (16) .... the barrels in the pit. These poles are used to turn the barrels and prevent the growth of scum (17) .... the mixture.

The paragraph you have just completed describes the parts of the methane digester according to their place or relationship to each other in space. This kind of description is called *spatial order*. Chronological order is arranged according to time. Spatial order is arranged according to spatial relationships. Many times, both descriptions are used in a paragraph, especially in descriptions of processes and procedures where directions are given (as in the preceding exercise). Both kinds of order are used in writing paragraphs about experiments. You can find elements of both chronological order and spatial order in the fill-in-the-blank exercise you have just completed.

Under the following headings, list the words from the paragraph that belong to each order:

Vocabulary of chronological order   *Vocabulary of spatial order*

....

....

....

....

....

....

....

Describe any object in a paragraph using spatial order. Draw a diagram with it.

Example The table I am describing is an object made of wood. It consists of a horizontal wooden surface which rests on four vertical, narrow, rectangular pieces of wood.

....

....

....

....

....

....

....

....

Vocabulary

Fill in the blanks with words from the vocabulary.

1. The prisoner wanted to get out of prison. He tried to .... at night.

2. One of the problems with heart transplants is that the body tries

   to .... the foreign organ. It doesn't want to keep it inside.

3. It is best to do a job .... instead of doing it quickly and carelessly.

4. The generator did not .... properly, so experts were called in to fix it.

5. Winter clothes may be .... with wool or fur.

6. Some chemicals will explode if they are .... It is best not to move them around too often.

7. Make-up can .... a woman's beauty. It can make her more beautiful than before.

8. We cannot .... people from over-using fossil fuels. However, we can make them understand our point of view.

9. The animal fell into the .... dug by the hunter.

10. Boats don't .... in water; they float.

CHAPTER 12

Vocabulary

windmill	to pump	to rotate
century	to spread	propeller
to transform	art	proportional
labour	to advance	cube
labour-saving	to drive (a machine)	square
to grind	exception	output

Affixes

I Prefixes

  A *Trans* – across, change

  B Prefixes of number

Grammar

 I Introductory paragraphs

 II Observations

Reading 12: Wind power (Part 1)

(1) Windmills have been used for centuries to transform the energy from the wind into labor-saving mechanical work, especially grinding grain and pumping water. (2) The use of windmills spread from Iran in the seventh century A.D. to China where the art of making windmills was advanced further. (3) Now, thirteen centuries later, we are again realizing the possibilities of using wind power. (4) The materials and technology are greatly improved, but the basic idea remains the same.

(5) All forms of usable electricity come from some type of rotating generator which is driven by an external power source. (6) The wind generator is no exception. (7) A wind-driven generator consists of a rotating generator turned by a propeller which is pushed around by the force of the wind upon it. (8) The propeller is like an engine using wind as its only fuel.

(9) The amount of electricity that can be generated by a wind generator is dependent on four things: the amount of wind blowing on it, the diameter of the propeller, the size of the generator, and the efficiency of the whole system. (10) The actual power available from the wind is proportional to the cube of the wind speed. (11) In other words, if you double the wind speed, you will get eight times as much power. (12) In addition, the power is proportional to the square of the diameter of the propeller. (13) By doubling the size of the propeller, we can increase the output by a factor of four. (14) These are the relationships which are basic in the design of any wind-driven power plant.

Worksheet

Sentence 1

A *windmill* is a machine that provides power through the rotation of propellers by the wind.
A *century* is one hundred years.
To transform something means to change it from one form to another.
Labor means work. *Labor-saving* means work-saving.
To grind something is to reduce it to powder.
To pump water means to bring water up from the ground.

1. A paraphrase of sentence (1) is:
   (a) Windmills have used people for many centuries. These centuries have changed the wind into grain and water. ☐
   (b) People have used windmills for many centuries. These windmills changed the energy from the wind to energy to do work. ☐
   (c) People have been used by windmills for many centuries. These windmills have changed the energy from the wind to energy to do work. ☐
   (d) None of the above. ☐

Sentence 2

To spread means to extend over a larger area.
Art means skill.
To advance means to step forward; to improve.

Paragraph (1) is an introduction to what follows in the story. It is an *introductory paragraph*. It gives the reader information and hints about what the remainder of the story will contain. It introduces some of the ideas that will be brought up later in the story. Sometimes an introductory paragraph gives background information about the main idea such as some history. It may also define or explain ideas that are basic to understanding a story, or it may simply be a summary of the major ideas to be covered in the story. In Reading (12), the introductory paragraph tells us some background history of windmills. It also gives us an idea of what the remainder of the story will be about.

1. The remainder of the story will probably be about:
   (a) The new technology of windmills ☐
   (b) The basic ideas behind the technology of windmills ☐

(c) Grinding grain ☐
(d) The relations between Iran and China ☐
(e) (a) and (b) ☐

Sentence 5

To drive a machine means to provide power to that machine.

Sentence 6

An *exception* is something that is not included in the general rule. 'It is no exception' means that it is not different.

1. A summary of sentences (5) and (6) is:
   (a) The wind generator is like other generators in that it produces usable electricity but it is unlike other generators in that it is exceptional. ☐
   (b) The wind generator isn't like other generators which produce electricity. It has a rotating generator but it is not powered by an external source. ☐
   (c) The wind generator is like other generators which produce electricity. It has a rotating generator. This generator receives its power from an outside source. ☐
   (d) None of the above. ☐

Sentence 7

To rotate means to turn.
A *propeller* is the part of a windmill that catches the wind.

1. Which is the correct time sequence for the workings of a wind-driven generator?

   (a) First, the wind rotates the generator. Then, the rotating generator turns a propeller. ☐
   (b) First, the wind turns a propeller. Then, the propeller turns a generator. ☐
   (c) First, the rotating generator turns a propeller. Then, the propeller catches the wind. ☐
   (d) None of the above. ☐

Sentence 8

1. A paraphrase of sentence (8) is:
   (a) The propeller has an engine which uses only wind and no other fuel. ☐
   (b) The propeller is like an engine in that it only uses fossil fuels. ☐

(c) The propeller is like an engine which is powered by wind
     in the same way that other engines are powered by gas
     or water.   ☐

(d) None of the above.   ☐

Sentence 9

1. A paraphrase of 'The amount of electricity that can be generated
    by a wind generator is dependent on four things' is:
    (a) We should take into account four things in order to judge
         how much electricity a wind generator can generate.   ☐
    (b) Four things can be generated by a wind generator to
         produce the amount of electricity we need.   ☐
    (c) Four things depend on a wind generator to generate
         amounts of electricity.   ☐
    (d) None of the above.   ☐

PARAGRAPH 3

If x is *proportional* to y, the ratio is x:y. If x is proportional to the *square*
of y, the ratio is $x:y^2$. If x is proportional to the *cube* of y, the ratio is
$x:y^3$.
Output means quantity produced; amount produced.

Which question best summarizes the third paragraph?
    (a) What is the energy production of a wind-driven generator
         dependent on?
    (b) How can we build a wind-driven generator?
    (c) What are the mathematical relationships between energy pro-
         duction and the wind?

Outline

Write your answer to the question about paragraph (3) (above) in the space next to III. *Fill in the rest of the blanks with information from paragraph (3).*

III ....

    A The amount of wind blowing on it

        1. ....

           (a) If you double the wind speed, you will get eight times as much power.

    B ....

        1. Power is proportional to the square of the diameter of the propeller.

           (a) ....

    C ....

    D ....

Vocabulary

Fill in the gaps with words from the vocabulary.

1. Through hard work, he .... himself from a poor student into an excellent student.

2. Modern inventions have given the housewife many .... machines such as washing machines and dishwashers.

3. These machines were invented during the last two .... Perhaps this is also why our energy use has increased in the past 200 years.

4. It takes a lot of human .... to .... water and

   .... grain.
5. Nowadays, most men don't do that work. The man who does that

   work himself is the .... to the general rule.

6. For most students, the quantity learned is .... to the time spent studying.

7. The .... of a solar powered construction depends partly on its geographic location.

8. The .... of making paper by hand is gradually disappearing. Most paper is now made by machine.

Prefixes

The word *transform* contains the prefix *trans-*. *Trans-* means across; change. *Transform* means to change from one form to another. Other words with the prefix *trans-* are:

transfer   – to change from one place to another
transplant – to lift and reset a plant into different soil; to lift and reset
                    anything into a different place
translate   – to change from one language to another
transpose – to change from one position to another
transport   – to carry from one place (across) to another

Other prefixes show numbers, such as in *century* and *decade*.

Prefix	Example	Meaning
micro-	micrometer (instrument for measuring very small objects)	one millionth 10^{-6} very small
hemi-	hemisphere (half of a sphere)	half
semi-	semicircle (half of a circle)	half
uni-	to unify (to make into one)	one
mono-	monotone (one sound)	one
bi-	bicycle	two
tri-	tricycle	three
quad-	quadrangle (something with four angles)	four
pent-	pentangle (something with five angles)	five
quint-	quintuplet (one of five children born at the same time from the same mother)	five
hex-	hexagon (six-sided shape)	six
sex-	sextuplet (one of six children born at the same time from the same mother)	six
hept-	heptagon (seven-sided shape)	seven
oct-	octagon (eight-sided shape)	eight
non-	nonagon (nine-sided shape)	nine
dec-	decimeter (one-tenth of a meter) decade (ten years)	ten
cent-	centimeter (one-hundredth of a meter) centennial (100 year marker) century (length of 100 years)	one hundred
mill-	millimeter (one thousandth of a meter) millenium (length of 1000 years)	one thousand
multi-	multicolored (many colours)	many

What do you think a unicycle is?

....

A *biped* is something that walks on two legs. What is a *quadruped*?

....

Something that is *trilateral* has three sides. How would you describe

something that has two sides? ....

Someone who speaks two languages is *bilingual*. What would you

call someone who speaks three languages? ....

Someone who speaks many languages? ....

The prefix *semi-* is often put in front of an adjective to show part or a
lesser degree of that adjective. For example, *semi-liquid* means part
liquid, part solid. *Semi-sweet* means not very sweet; slightly sweet.

Semidangerous means ....

Semiskilled means .... *Semi-*

opaque means .... (*Opaque*
means not transparent. We cannot see through something that is

opaque. No light comes through.) *Semi-literate* means ....

.... (*Literate* means able to
read.)

Grammar—observations

Look at sentence (12) in the reading: 'If you double the wind speed, you will get eight times as much power.' We can divide this sentence into two parts. The first part is the *instruction*: 'Double the wind speed.' The second part is the *result*. 'You will get eight times as much power.'

When we combine an instruction and a result into one sentence with *if* or *when*, we form an *observation*. Thus, some possible observations are:

1. If you double the wind speed, you will get eight times as much power.
2. You will get eight times as much power if you double the wind speed.
3. If the wind speed is doubled, you will get eight times as much power.
4. You will get eight times as much power if the wind speed is doubled.
5. When you double the wind speed, you will get eight times as much power.
6. You will get eight times as much power when you double the wind speed.
7. When the wind speed is doubled, you will get eight times as much power.
8. You will get eight times as much power when the wind speed is doubled.

In each sentence there is an instruction clause and a result clause. *If* or *when* always come before the instruction clause.

Another way to state an observation is in these forms:

9. By doubling the wind speed, you get eight times as much power.
10. You get eight times as much power by doubling the wind speed.

Sentence (14) is in form 9, above. Sentence (13) is also an observation. Which is the instruction clause in sentence (13)?

.... Which is the result clause

in (13)? ....

152

We can also write sentence (13) like this: If we double the size of the propeller, we can increase the output by a factor of four.

Write four more possible ways to state this observation.

....

....

....

....

....

....

....

....

....

....

....

Match the correct instruction and result to form a logical observation.

Instructions	Results
1. Heat water to 100°C.	(a) It will burn.
2. Drop a weight from a height of two feet.	(b) It will form carbon dioxide.
3. Apply a match to a piece of paper.	(c) It will boil.
4. Combine one part of carbon to two parts of oxygen.	(d) It will cause pollution.
5. Throw waste products in a river.	(e) It will fall.

Write two observations for each correct instruction-result combination. Use each form only once.

Example 1. If we heat water to 100°C, it will boil.
2. Water will boil if we heat it to 100°C.

Continue the rest.

3. ....

....

....

4. ....

....

....

5. ....

....

....

6. ....

....

....

7. ....

....

....

8. ....

....

....

9. ....

....

....

10. ....

....

....

CHAPTER 13

Vocabulary

applicable	minimal	rod
to perfect	to split	to insert
minimum	to offset	to expose

Skills

Outlining 'how-to' directions from a reading passage

Reading 13: Wind power (Part 2)

(1) Windmills, which are driven by arm-like propellers, are the most basic and most widespread uses of wind power. (2) The wind-powered grain mills in Holland are of this kind. (3) Another type of wind-powered construction which is less perfected but possibly more applicable to smaller projects, is called the S-Rotor generator. (4) It can be built with a minimum of supplies and a minimal amount of money.

(5) To begin building the S-Rotor generator, a cylinder is split into two equal halves lengthwise. (6) Secondly, these halves are offset by a distance approximately equal to the radius of the original cylinder. (See the diagram of the 'offset' or 'split' cylinder.) (7) Next, these halves are attached to metal sheets which are as large as the new diameter. (8) Subsequently, a rod is inserted through the center of the new construction. (9) Then the ends of the rods are fixed into bearings so that the construction can rotate when exposed to the wind. (10) Finally, gears, alternators, and battery systems are attached underneath the three cylinders.

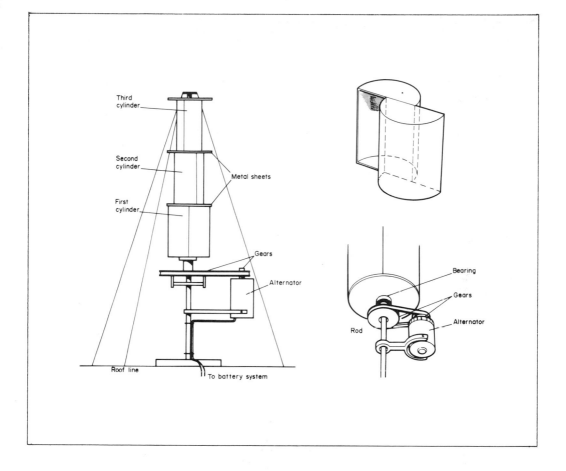

Worksheet

Sentence 2

1. 'This kind' refers to:
   (a) The kind that is driven by arm-like propellers
   (b) The kind that is less perfected and called the S-Rotor generator
   (c) The kind that is the most basic and most widespread use of wind power
   (d) (a) and (c)
   (e) None of the above

Sentence 3

Applicable means able to be applied; can be used.
To perfect something is to make it better.

Sentence 4

A *minimum* is a small amount. *Minimal* means small.

PARAGRAPH 1
What are some *advantages* of the S-Rotor generator over wind-mills?
- (a) They are less perfected, are more applicable to smaller projects, and can be built with a minimum of supplies and a minimal amount of money. ☐
- (b) They are more applicable to smaller projects, can be built with a minimum of supplies and a minimal amount of money, and use only fossil fuels. ☐
- (c) They are more applicable to smaller projects, and can be built with a minimum of supplies and a minimal amount of money. ☐
- (d) None of the above. ☐

Sentence 5

To split means to divide.

Sentence 8

To insert something is to put it inside of another thing.
A *rod* is a pole.

Sentence 9

To be exposed means to be in view; to be in the open; to be subject to something.

PARAGRAPH 2
Circle all the words that show chronological order.

Giving directions *Look at the diagram closely. Use words from the list below to complete the following sentences. Use each word only once.*

exterior	above	horizontally	interior
between	vertically	adjacent to	below
to the right	on the surface	at the bottom	

1. The second cylinder is .... the first and third cylinders.

2. The rod is placed .... through the cylinders.

3. The .... of the cylinders is empty.

4. The alternator, the battery system, and the gears are ....
the cylinders.

5. The base of the S-Rotor is .... of the roof.

6. The alternator is .... of the rod.

7. The S-Rotor system is .... the ground.

Using paragraph 2 as a guide, write a series of directions on how to build an S-Rotor generator. Number the directions (1) to (6). Remember that directions are in the command form. They do not need vocabulary of chronological order because they are numbered.

How to build an S-Rotor generator

1. ....

2. ....

3. ....

4. ....

5. ....

6. ....

CHAPTER 14

Vocabulary

to compare	nature	to align
wind tunnel tests	prevalent	to swing
inferior	gust	to absorb
superior	to deviate	asset

Vocabulary of comparison and contrast

Affixes

Prefixes co- (two or more together) and its variations

Grammar

Paragraphs of comparison and contrast

Reading 14: Wind power (Part 3)

(1) How does the S-Rotor generator compare with the windmill in efficiency? (2) If the wind tunnel tests of the two systems are compared, the S-Rotor generator appears inferior. (3) However, under normal wind conditions, the results are nearly the same.

(4) To understand why this occurs, we should take a closer look at the nature of wind. (5) There are two basic types of wind: the prevalent wind and the energy wind. (6) The former blows on an average of five days out of seven days while the latter blows only on the remaining two days out of seven. (7) Energy winds come in the form of strong gusts so that approximately 70 percent of the energy comes from energy winds which blow only 30 percent of the time. (8) One characteristic of these energy winds is that they usually deviate in direction from a prevalent wind by fifteen to seventeen degrees. (9) At the time of these gusts, the windmill loses much of the energy from both the gust and the steady wind that follows because it needs time to align itself with the two winds. (10) The S-Rotor generator, however, is able to absorb the full energy of both the gust and the steady wind because it doesn't have to 'swing'. (11) One of the greatest assets of the S-Rotor generator, then, is that it can take a wind from any direction at any time. (12) However, in places where the difference between energy winds and prevalent winds is minimal, where the wind comes mostly from the same direction, or where the wind is fairly weak, a windmill will provide more power.

Worksheet

Sentence 1

To compare things is to show the similarities and differences between things.

Sentence 2

Wind tunnel tests are tests to determine the effect of air pressure on an object. The object is placed in a passageway through which air is blown at a known velocity.

1. Another way to say: 'The object is placed in a passageway through which air is blown at a known velocity' is:
    (a) The object is placed in a passageway which blows air at a known velocity through. ☐
    (b) The object is placed in a passageway. The passageway blows through air at a known velocity. ☐
    (c) The object is placed in a passageway which air is blown through at a known velocity. ☐
    (d) (b) and (c). ☐
    (e) None of the above. ☐

Inferior means worse.
Superior means better.

Sentence 4

The *nature* of something means its basic characteristics.

Sentence 5

Prevalent means widespread.

Sentence 6

1. 'The former' refers to ....

   'The latter' refers to ....

Sentence 7

A *gust* is a sudden burst of wind. If the wind speed changes suddenly from 10 m.p.h. to 50 m.p.h. and then back to 10 m.p.h., we call the 50 m.p.h. a *gust*.

1. Energy winds blow .... percent of the time; however, they

   provide .... percent of wind energy. Prevalent winds blow

   .... percent of the time; however, they only provide .... percent of the wind energy.

Sentence 8

To deviate means to change away from the usual.

Sentence 9

To align means to move into line.

Sentence 10

To absorb means to take in.
To swing means to move from one side to another.

Sentence 11

An *asset* is a benefit; an advantage.

Reading comprehension *Answer these questions about the whole reading.*

1. In this story, ... and .... are compared in efficiency.
   (a) A wind-driven generator, a solar powered generator ☐
   (b) An S-Rotor generator, a windmill ☐
   (c) A man, a woman ☐
   (d) None of the above ☐

2. If we did these tests in a wind tunnel, which would seem most efficient?
   (a) The solar powered generator ☐
   (b) The windmill ☐
   (c) The S-Rotor generator ☐
   (d) The woman ☐

3. Is the wind-tunnel test always the best way to judge a construction?

   .... Why?
   (a) No. The conditions in a wind tunnel are not always the same as conditions in real life. ☐
   (b) Yes. The conditions in a wind tunnel are exactly the same as in real life. ☐
   (c) Yes. In the wind tunnel, the wind is always at the same velocity. ☐
   (d) (b) and (c). ☐
   (e) None of the above. ☐

4. Under what conditions can an S-Rotor generator be more efficient than a windmill?
   (a) If there is a large deviation in direction between the gusts and prevalent winds ☐
   (b) If the wind comes mostly from the same direction ☐
   (c) If the wind is not strong ☐
   (d) (a) and (b) ☐
   (e) None of the above ☐

5. Why does the S-Rotor generator have an advantage when there is a large deviation between gusts and prevalent winds?
   (a) It does not need time to align itself for each new wind. ☐
   (b) It doesn't have to 'swing' to catch wind from different directions. ☐
   (c) It has openings in the cylinders in all directions to catch the wind. ☐
   (d) All of the above. ☐

6. To summarize the comparison between the efficiency of an S-Rotor generator and a windmill, we can say:
   (a) The S-Rotor is superior in a wind-tunnel test but the windmill may be superior under real life conditions. The S-Rotor works better than the windmill when there is a large deviation in direction between gusts and prevalent winds. The windmill works better than the S-Rotor when the wind is fairly weak and where there is not too great a difference between gusts and prevalent winds. ☐
   (b) There are gusts and prevalent winds when we use the S-Rotor generator. When we use windmills, the wind is at a known velocity. ☐
   (c) The S-Rotor generator is inferior in wind-tunnel tests but it may be superior under certain real life conditions,

such as when there is a large difference between the direction of gusts and the direction of prevalent winds and when the wind is generally strong.

(d) None of the above.

Vocabulary

Fill in the blanks with words from the vocabulary.

1. Some people think that men are .... to women. They think that men are better.

2. Most people follow what everyone else does. They don't want to do anything unusual. It is hard for them to .... from the norm (the usual way).

3. A .... blew the man's hat 20 feet into the air.

4. He will be an .... to your company. He works hard and will do your business a lot of good.

5. My car kept going to the right. I couldn't drive straight. The mechanic said I had to .... the wheels.

6. Disease is .... in places where sewage is not disposed of properly. Many people get sick.

Paragraphs of Comparison and Contrast

So far we have looked at three types of paragraph:
1. A paragraph which has an introductory topic sentence and remaining sentences in a chronological order.
2. A paragraph which has a generalizing topic sentence and remaining sentences which justify it by giving examples or details.
3. A paragraph which has an introductory topic sentence and remaining sentences in a spatial order (or a combination of spatial and chronological order).

Reading 14 was an example of another type of paragraph:

4. A paragraph with a topic sentence which introduces a comparison or contrast. The remaining sentences give details, examples, background, etc., about this comparison.

A *comparison* looks at the differences and similarities between two things.
A *contrast* generally looks at the differences between two things.

Order the following sentences to form paragraphs contrasting or comparing some idea. Circle the words in the sentences which help show comparisons or contrasts.

Group 1

.... Just as Riyadh is the center of education and business in Saudi Arabia, so Paris is the center of education and business in France.

.... On the other hand, Riyadh has a much smaller population than Paris.

.... Riyadh and Paris are similar in some respects and dissimilar in other respects.

.... Physically, too, Riyadh differs from Paris.

.... First of all, they resemble each other in that they are both capital cities and therefore, both contain government offices.

.... Riyadh is surrounded by desert whereas Paris is surrounded by flat, green land.

Group 2

.... For one thing, they both come from Latin.

.... In contrast, French has both masculine and feminine words whereas English doesn't.

.... The English language and the French language have many things in common.

.... For another thing, the English *f* often corresponds to the French p.

Group 3

.... Other criteria for comparison are effort, class participation, and homework.
.... On a test where 70 is the highest grade, perhaps the student who gets the 70 should get an A.

.... On other tests, however, where the highest grade is 100, students with 70s should probably get Cs.

.... One method of computing students' grades is to compare students.

Vocabulary of comparison and contrast includes the following:

to be similar to = to have something in common with = to have characteristics in common with = to have a resemblance to = to resemble
similarly = likewise = in a like manner = in the same way
just as . . . so is . . .
to correspond to = to have a correspondence with = to relate to = to have a relationship with = to be parallel to

to be unlike = to be dissimilar to = to differ from = to be different from
dissimilarly
on the other hand = in contrast = on the contrary = whereas

Use words from the Vocabulary of comparison and contrast *above to fill in the blanks in the following sentences:*

1. Solar energy is .... wind energy in that they are both alternative energy sources.

2. .... solar energy is an alternative source of energy,

   .... energy from the wind an alternative source of energy.

3. Solar energy is an alternative source of energy. ...., energy from the wind is an alternative energy source.

4. Solar energy is .... energy from fossil fuels in that solar energy does not pollute whereas fossil fuels do.

5. Solar energy cannot be exhausted .... fossil fuels can.

Prefix co-

The words *compare* and *contrast* both contain the prefix *co-* (*co-* changes to *com-, con-, col-* and *cor-* depending on the letter following it). The prefix means two or more together.

Cooperate means to work together.
To compare means to show the similarities and differences between two or more things.
To correlate means to relate two or more things.
To collaborate means to work together with others on one project.
A *contract* is an agreement between two or more people.

Final project

Go to the library and look up the plans for some simple project using ideas of appropriate technology. In the description of the project, and in the directions or plans for building the project, mark the parts that show chronological order or spatial order. If this project is an improvement or variation of a similar project, mark the parts which contrast or compare the two designs. Remember that *all* paragraphs do not contain *all* of these constructions, but you should be able to find some examples in any project description.

Bring the plans to class and describe the project to the other students. Discuss whether the plan is feasible. Discuss where the project would be most appropriate.

Notes: